STATES OF THE BODY
PRODUCED BY LOVE

STATES OF THE BODY
PRODUCED BY LOVE

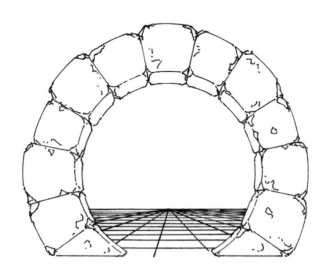

BY NISHA RAMAYYA

First published by Ignota 2019
© Nisha Ramayya 2019

The moral rights of the author have been asserted.

Ignota has attempted to contact all copyright holders.
We apologise for any omissions, and if notified we will amend in future editions.

1 3 5 7 9 10 8 6 4 2

ISBN-13: 978-1-9996759-4-3

Cover detail: Chinnamastā
Anonymous painting from Rajasthan, c. 18th century.
Design by Cecilia Serafini
Typeset in Adobe Garamond by Iram Allam
Printed and bound in Great Britain by TJ International

For my family –

For Mum, Papa and Gaurav

For Shalini maasi, Sanjiv uncle and Devika

For Ramesh uncle, Sandhya chaachi, Ashwin and Tarun

For Dadi

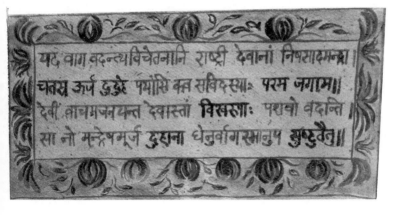

Contents

1 The Goddess Disappears Underground   1

2 'Is she anywhere after this, is she too far for us?'   16

From *Notes on Sanskrit*   17
    In the Rainstorm   17
    Out of the Throat   21
    Little Mothers   22
    The Lexicographer-Priest   24
    Notes on Sanskrit   27

From *Correspondences*   31
    Notes on Tantra   31
    Ritual Steps for a Tantric Poetics   34
    Correspondence as Writing System   36
    Correspondence as Make Believe   37
    Make Believe as Sacrifice   38
    Her Voice as an Instrument of Thought   39
    Correspondence as a Compass on the Body   44

Thirteen Days after Death   46

3 States of the Body Produced by Love   53

Joy of the Eyes   54
Pensive Reflection   55
Desire   56

Sleeplessness   57
Emaciation   59
Indifference to External Objects   60
Abandonment of Shame   62
Infatuation   70
Fainting Away   78
Death   84

we are seen by the world / what must be seen   89

Futures Flowers   92

4 Love's Future Is Death   96

Notes on References   108

Works Cited in Order of Appearance   116

Acknowledgements   119

The Goddess Disappears Underground

1

Begin with Kamala (lotus flower), the tenth Mahāvidyā; hail Lakṣmī (the good sign), Gajalakṣmī (elephantine fortune), Amṛta (one who is not dead, nectar, residue of the sacrifice).

She is the antidote to poison; she is the poison itself. She is the poison – state-sanctioned documents, honorific prefix, holding a lotus she rose to the top. She is the poison – foaming progress, betray (profane), rosy or safflower dominion. She is the poison – four white elephants, conferring immortality, produced at the churning of the ocean. This is not where I want to begin.

Begin with honey love and family homes, every other holiday spent in India (holidays are constitutive: time in India vivifies time not-in-India, as time in Scotland vivifies time not-in-Scotland; *missing something* makes me feel at home); growing up with my family's memories, my inability to separate myself from my family's memories, to disentangle our versions of India, our dreams of the future. Begin with the yellow-leafed view of things seen from a distance, as seen between seasons, as seen through the stickiness of an unclean break; hail Śrī (mixing, cooking, diffusing light).

Begin with the possibility of this break never ending, of the endless possibilities of return; hail Aditi (not tied, free, boundless, 'Eternal and Infinite Expanse'). The names of deities are points on a map; utter your flight paths home.

*

Fall in love with the Mahāvidyās; learn their names, translate their stories, make the shapes of their hands with your hands.

*

Translated from Sanskrit, *mahā-vidyā* is great or full knowledge, skill, incantation. As *vidyā* also denotes a grammatically feminine mantra, knowledge of the Mahāvidyās is a specifically linguistic and literary capacity. As mantras, the Mahāvidyās embody language – they are words, actions, meanings, and the supreme stage of language that transcends words, actions, meanings. They speak me into being; I cannot precede myself to translate their stories into my own words.

The ten goddesses are diverse embodiments of one supreme Goddess, as David Kinsley explains: 'All of the Mahāvidyās are the same: they are all different expressions of the same goddess, who enjoys taking many forms for her own pleasure and the needs of her devotees.' They include some of the oldest, most popular and most obscure goddesses in Hindu and Buddhist traditions, and are worshipped as individual deities as part of those traditions and as a group within their own Tantric Hindu tradition. There is no single explanation for the grouping of these goddesses, which took place sometime in the tenth century. However, there are multiple origin myths, all of which identify the goddesses as *avatāras* of Śakti: mainly Satī, but also Pārvatī, Durgā and Kālī. (The Mahāvidyās are associated with Śiva, although the Śiva/Śakti dynamic varies for each goddess.)

Satī is the symbol of what Christian missionaries in India called 'certain Dreadful Practices' – namely, widow-burning – denounced in the early nineteenth century by Bengali reformer Raja Rammohan Roy, whose pamphlets were published in English. *Sati* was a source of shame for Roy and his peers, who were 'eager to counteract the missionary view that Indians were barbarous and uncivilized, and referred to "cruel murder, under the cloak of religion" which had led to Indians being regarded with "contempt and pity . . . by all civilized nations on the surface of the globe."' Of course, 'civilized nations' have their own traditions of gendered violence, under the cloak of religion and wearing the well-shined badge of the state (witch trials; Magdalene Laundries; Missing and Murdered Indigenous Women, Girls and 2SQ People; death in custody, death in prison; the violence coterminous with the 'Trans Tipping Point'), but some nations wear their shame more lightly than others. *Sati* was criminalised in 1829 and still makes headlines.

When a Lovely Flame Dies

Satī's story begins in the early days of the world. Brahmā (the impersonal one) was tired of creation; he created Dakṣa (dextrous) from the thumb of his right hand to populate the world. Dakṣa had many children, but none compared to Satī. She was a good and faithful woman, an ascetic, and her father loved her the most.

Today the Hindu pantheon is made of three: Brahmā, Viṣṇu, Śiva, and their consorts Sarasvatī, Lakṣmī and Pārvatī. Hindus worship Viṣṇu, Śiva and the Goddess in numerous denominational and regional forms. In the time of this story, the pantheon had not been constructed. Śiva was an outsider (possibly of non-Vedic origin) and had not been granted the position that he now enjoys. No one doubted his power, but they sensed something demonic about him. So when Satī announced her intention to wed Śiva, Dakṣa was furious:

He lives in the burning ground surrounded by *pretas* [ghosts], *bhūtas* [good or evil spirits] and *piśācas* [ogres]. With his hair all matted and wild he wanders naked in the burning ground. He laughs awhile and weeps awhile like one demented. He smears himself with the ashes from the funeral pyre and wears a garland made of human skulls.

Dakṣa refused to give Satī his permission until his own father intervened; he assented but withheld his blessing. He hosted a great sacrificial ceremony on the banks of the Ganga, inviting everyone in all the realms, except Satī and Śiva. When Satī heard about the ceremony, she was hurt that Dakṣa had excluded her and embarrassed that he had offended Śiva. She was determined to attend, but Śiva, as guilty as his father-in-law of prideful behaviour, refused to accompany her. He tried to dissuade her, they argued, and she left.

When Satī arrived at the ceremony, she confronted Dakṣa:

'I am defiled by your arrogance, father. I should have stayed with my husband, for now I cannot return to him. I am still your daughter, your flesh and blood, though I would not be. O evil father, how I hate myself that I am your child!'

Her eyes blazed, and she said, 'Look, I cast off this body born from your loins as if it were a corpse. I shall be my Lord's wife again when I am born to a father I can love.'

Satī concentrated her power on *tapas*, the religious austerity that sears mind and soul with purifying heat. But her *tapas* was so powerful that she lit a fire inside her body and burned to death from within. Satī's hollow ash-filled corpse remained upright as a pillar to her father's mistake: 'You cannot live without performing sacrifice but I am the sacrifice.'

Meditating on Mount Kailāśa, Śiva knew what had happened. He unleashed his devastation in the form of the fever-demon Vīrabhadra, and Dakṣa's ceremony became the site of a massacre. The world was almost destroyed that day but *dharma* (according to the nature of anything; Law or Justice) prevented it: a ceremony must be concluded. Śiva sacrificed Vīrabhadra and distributed his fire among the gods. For good measure, he transformed Dakṣa's head into the head of a goat: 'Dakṣa was now freed of his proud and arrogant nature and he was a highly chastened person. Only, Satī was dead.'

Satī's body remained through all of this, and when Śiva was done, he took hold of her and wept and ran madly across the world, causing a different kind of destruction. Viṣṇu, who had been conspicuously quiet, was drawn into the story to alleviate Śiva's grief. He threw his discus and cut Satī's body into fifty pieces (this number is debated). These pieces fell to earth and became sacred sites known as *Śaktipīṭhas*. The map of South Asia is a map of Satī's love for Śiva, a map of a good woman's duty to her husband. The goddess sacrificed herself so that the gods could come to an agreement over their positions in the pantheon. It was clear that Śiva was too powerful to ignore, and his wildness was assimilated and authorised. Satī was reincarnated as Pārvatī, daughter of the mountain, and remarried to Śiva. *Dharma* was restored.

The story of Dakṣa and Śiva's conflict is recounted in several sacred texts, including the *Mahābhārata*; although Satī is a key figure, no mention is made of her corpse. Shaktism corrects this omission, describing the *Śaktipīṭhas* in the *Devībhāgavata Purāṇa*. Tantric Hindu myths revise the story substantially, emphasising the power and agency of the goddess in the *Mahābhāgavata Purāṇa* and the *Bṛhaddharma Purāṇa*. Returning to the moment that Śiva forbids Satī from leaving their home, this version conveys her reaction:

Her eyes become red and bright and her limbs tremble. Seeing her fury, Śiva closes his eyes. When he opens them, a fearsome female stands before him . . . Śiva is afraid and tries to flee. He runs around in all directions, but then the terrible goddess gives a dreadful laugh, and Śiva is too petrified to move. To make sure that he does not flee from her terrible form, Satī fills the directions around him with ten different forms.

The Mahāvidyās embody Satī's anger towards the men in her life (the men who claim to love her), her refusal to be determined in relation to them or on their terms, her powers of transformation and the potential of her symbolic dominance beyond the limits of her own myth. The image of Satī filling the directions around Śiva reminds me of an image in Ambedkar's *Annihilation of Caste*: '[The revolutionary] will be compelled to take account of caste after the revolution, if he does not take account of it before the revolution. This is only another way of saying that, turn in any direction you like, caste is the monster that crosses your path.' I am guilty of conflating images. It's like saying: be the monster that must be sacrificed; kill the monster that you are.

The Mahāvidyās are metaphors, which is where the difficulty begins. If I'm not careful, I allow them to mean everything, to make everything possible, to swallow the whole world so that I can't see anything without looking through her, without piercing the skin of her feminist context. I don't want to pierce her in order to realise what exists beyond her; I must eat her first.

*

Fall in love, realise love's treachery, work my way backwards from joy of the eyes.

2

Begin with Mātaṅgī, the ninth Mahāvidyā. The outcaste goddess, she has jungle green skin and long unkempt hair. She wears red clothes decorated with red jewels, forest flowers and shells that glow in the dark. She smiles, her eyes swivelling with intoxication, her face perspiring brightly. Her clothes hang loosely in her drunken state, revealing too much of her breasts, too much of the hair on her body. She is the base goddess; rough as elephant hide, regal in her own way.

Begin with Samuel Johnson and his dictionary. In the preface, he confesses an initial desire to 'fix' or 'embalm' the language. Johnson invokes a language that is organic matter – a mutable, multiplying language that would be improved by the stasis of death. He defines 'embalm' as: 'To impregnate a body with aromaticks, that it may resist putrefaction', illustrating the definition with reference to part of this passage from Shakespeare's *Henry VIII*:

When I am dead, good wench,
Let me be used with honour. Strew me over
With maiden flowers, that all the world may know
I was a chaste wife to my grave. Embalm me,

Then lay me forth. Although unqueened, yet like
A queen and daughter to a king inter me.

Mātaṅgī is queen of the elephants. Elephants symbolise civil
and martial authority: 'the owning of elephants, it appears, was
a prerogative of kings.' But Mātaṅgī does not own elephants, she
moves with them. They clear paths for each other through the
jungle – elephants crashing through the tangle, Mātaṅgī wielding
her divine powers 'to vanquish every obstacle of the Way.' Elephants
are not without divine powers of their own; they were once winged
companions to the clouds and retain the ability to communicate
with their 'celestial relatives'. This relationship is now more or
less forgotten. Cries for rain, for fertility, for verdure go unheard;
elephants wait to be asked.

Mātaṅgī reels through the jungle, singing loudly, doing as she
pleases. Her name translates as 'going wilfully' or 'roaming at will',
and is a synonym for 'elephant' and 'cloud'. Sara Ahmed discusses
the wilful subject: 'The wilful character insists on willing their own
way, without reference to reason or command. Wilfulness could be
described as a character perversion: to be wilful is to deviate, to will
one's own way is to will the wrong way.'

Mātaṅgī deviates, flaunting her talents in the margins of Hindu
mythology. Like Sarasvatī, she plays the *vīṇā* (Indian lute); she
plucks the strings of a community of her own making, like Sappho.
She is stagger and sweat, answering to earth, eroticism and the
sixty-four performance arts.

Wondering about her relationship with her silvery-white coun-
terpart Sarasvatī (she who once flowed), I remember a conversation
with my mother about satellite images:

myths are distributed
authored by atmosphere
the goddess disappears underground

rivers are tangled in nomenclature
Mātaṅgī, Prakṛti, Sarasvatī, Vāc

she blows out of course
subject to the curves of the shell

characterised by daring
boundless and destitute
her body contradicts the definition

coated in white petals, tide-bound
awaiting the synonymous burst

Imagining this explosion of lexicographical matter – 'the synon-
ymous burst' – I try to rest my mind, waiting for the thing that
happens next to come into focus. Johnson writes: 'It is remarkable
that, in reviewing my collection, I found the word *sea* unexempli-
fied.' His first definition of 'sea' is: 'The ocean; the water opposed to
the land.' The fourth entry is: 'Any thing rough and tempestuous.'

Ahmed describes the experience of going against the flow as
a feminist practice, struggling for change against the tide of the
social:

> We can note how the social can be experienced as a force: you
> can feel a force most directly when you attempt to resist it. It is
> the experience of 'coming up against' that is named by wilful-
> ness . . . wilfulness is a collecting together, of those struggling
> for a different ground for existence.

Mātaṅgī is the name of a community of outcaste women in South
India. Since the tenth century they have served as 'village shaman-
esses': '[They] will periodically become possessed by the goddess,
drinking toddy and dancing in a wild frenzy as they run about
spitting toddy on the assembled crowd, uttering strange wild cries
and hurling obscene verbal abuse at all present.'

Johnson's fifth entry is: '*Half* seas *over*. Half drunk.'

Mātaṅgī, outcaste goddess, the names of a river, the sea, 'rough
and tempestuous', wilful feminist, her eyes swivelling with intoxi-
cation . . . Am I forcing these connections, am I confusing contact

with commonality? Return to language, to Johnson's embalming practices. Place the body in an open space and sing her names.

अपारपार **apārapāra**, that which will not acquiesce

चण्डालिका **caṇḍālikā**, a woman of 'the lowest and most despised of the mixed tribes', born from a low-caste father and a high-caste mother (this term can also signify a menstruator)

मातङ्गी **mātaṅgī**, she whose limbs are exhilarated, intoxicated, inspired

Pollution and Power

Mātaṅgī is associated with those who do the dirtiest and most necessary work. She dwells with her devotees in forests, mountains, slums and cremation grounds. Unlike deities associated with higher castes, she gladly receives leftover food and rotten objects (including blood-stained clothes), which she reciprocates with blessings. Revelling in her status, she is assertively shameless. Her clothes smell of sweat, her fingernails and the soles of her feet are impacted with dirt, she laughs at the thought of a head bath every other day. Those who love her will never love her any less.

Ahmed uses Mary Douglas's definition of dirt as 'matter out of place' to examine the fear and hostility that accompanies the arrival of the foreign stranger. Matter out of place is an object or idea likely to 'confuse or contradict cherished classifications' – like dirt, like the alien in one's neighbourhood. Ahmed identifies the stranger as the body '*out of place*', whose skin is a mark of difference, a boundary that contains otherness and enables contact, '*a border that feels*':

> While the skin appears to be the matter which separates the body, it rather allows us to think of how the materialisation of bodies involves, not containment, but an affective opening out

of bodies to other bodies, in the sense that the skin registers how bodies are touched by others.

Mātaṅgī's skin is green like her wild environment, marking her at home in the jungle and out of place anywhere else. Her body is leaking and receptive; she sweats, she menstruates, she is sexually provocative. Like an aggressive bull elephant, she emits rut fluid.

Discussing the concept of 'stranger danger', Ahmed notes that the stranger is the origin of a multitude of possible dangers. The stranger is dangerous wherever she is – in public, in private and in the spaces through which she moves: 'spaces are claimed, or "owned" not so much by inhabiting what is already there, but by moving within, or passing through, different spaces which are only given value as places (with boundaries) through the movement or "passing through" itself.'

Mātaṅgī crosses boundaries; wherever she roams becomes slick with the feel of her. She emerges from and exists within greens and reds, leaving traces of representation in her wake. Mātaṅgī's pollution is social and spiritual disorder is the source of her power: 'The danger which is risked by boundary transgression is power. Those vulnerable margins and those attacking forces which threaten to destroy good order represent the powers inhering in the cosmos.'

Divine Abjection

Mātaṅgī is the menstruator who disregards her confines, who makes sexual propositions or otherwise abuses her temporary power. She is any person who violates socially imposed prohibitions, who wanders about encouraging others to disobey. As the goddess of pollution, she exemplifies the taboo – the sacred and the unclean, desirable and contagious, inciting veneration and revulsion. As the image of a marginalised yet empowered person, she represents the transgressive, that which cannot be repressed.

In *Powers of Horror*, Julia Kristeva describes the horror of the abject as the realisation that it comes from within. The borders between self and object, I and other, inside and outside, life and death are confounded by the abject, whose unsettling presence calls such oppositions into question. The horror of the abject triggers a sublime experience, 'a spree of perceptions and words that expands memory boundlessly' and leads into a 'secondary universe'. This experience is 'a divergence' and temporary transformation of the self.

This could be the experience of transforming into the Goddess, the expansion of consciousness to cosmic proportions. In Hindu traditions, the way to realise divinity most fully is to self-divinise, via worship, meditation and action. Tantra offers abundant points of entry into this process of transformation, empowering all sorts of people to know the way, including those who don't have the secret passwords and heirloom ritual tools, and who can't afford to pay. This apparently democratic approach to divinity might help to explain why Tantra is so appealing to some, so antagonistic to others.

After self-divinisation, the devotee returns to herself and to her community. She may remember the experience, she may retain some aspect of the transformation; for example, understanding the experience of being both and neither simultaneously. As Kristeva writes, 'Abjection is a resurrection that has gone through death (of the ego). It is an alchemy that transforms death drive into a start of life, of new significance.' But divinisation cannot remain, although abjection might; spiritually speaking, the devotee is now a corpse: 'death infecting life'. Her marginal, possibly contagious position in the community might return to her – painfully – after the ritual.

What Should We Do with the Body?
(The Body Is Not Just Language)

Who am I in relation to her, or rather, where? Mātaṅgī's sweat and slime, her greens and reds, her love of marginalised people and her emancipatory powers are metaphors. What are metaphors in relation to the material realities that they represent, condense, carry across, transform, displace, destroy and forget? Which menstruators does she represent; who is entitled to ask her for help; at what point does interest become appropriation? I come up against the desire to be literal. At this point in time, the Supreme Court of India is rejecting the vast majority of land claims under the Forest Rights Act and ordering the eviction of millions of local and Indigenous forest-dwelling people across the country, thereby dispossessing them of land, legal recognition and the ability to subsist. Today, as for hundreds of years, Indigenous people in Turtle Island face expropriation of land and resources, displacement and genocidal violence against nations, bodies and cultures. These are historically and geographically specific issues, certainly, but they are not discrete. The violence perpetrated by British colonialism on Indigenous people in India, North America and all over the world has created a complex of pain and destruction that overcomes the UK and Fortress Europe. The relationships between the experiences of those subjected to that colonial violence – directly, indirectly, globally and intergenerationally – are obscured by contemporary dominant narratives about borders, nationality and immigration, and the methods of their enactment. I read dissenting scholars and activists Édouard Glissant, Leanne Betasamosake Simpson, Don Mee Choi and Nat Raha, to ask: What is pensive reflection in a time of repeating crises – or rather, when?

3

Begin with Bagalāmukhī, the eighth Mahāvidyā; hail she who holds my tongue. Begin with her hurting hold, the love of origins; let her take the words out of my mouth, rivers, birds; return to the trap of my own words and practices; translate this trap to find her.

*

यन्त्र **yantra**, n. any instrument for holding or restraining or fastening; a fetter, band, tie, thong, rein, trace; any mechanical contrivance, engine, machine, appliance (as a bolt or lock on a door, oars or sails in a boat, &c.); a mystical diagram supposed to possess occult powers; my desire for her powers

4

Begin with Dhūmāvatī, the seventh Mahāvidyā. The smoke from Satī's burning body, her sacrifice, her fury.

*

Manu said: 'After her husband is dead, she may voluntarily emaciate her body by eating pure flowers, roots, and fruits; but she must never mention even the name of another man. Aspiring to that unsurpassed Law of women devoted to a single husband, she should remain patient, controlled, and celibate until her death.'

*

Documentary photography: Two small-to-medium dogs pose before a fire pit; the hounds of hell sit nicely. Blue smoke rises up a sandstone staircase, a rhododendron bush grows out of a pockmarked copper bowl. Brown skin dusted with ash to bring out its already ashy qualities; her head in the fire pit, white kurta slip. The pit again, the woman gone. Gold graduation jewellery engraved with smiling Lakṣmī; it's all that seems to remain of her. Handful of mud scooped out of mud, in which milk pools, lilac petals winking by banks. Ghee rumbles and mountains out of milk-pool, attracts mud; mud clings to ghee, irreducibly. Collaged black-and-white photographs of women, which means they are all dead. Several wear white, wear garlands of white flowers; monochrome emphasises this fiction of race. Almost all wearing bindis, almost none smiling. Cook butter soil mix. Two dogs pose at the top of the staircase, before a colourless sky. At the bottom, two poster-sized crows turn their heads. A woman washes her face in ash, Ella Fitzgerald playing in the background. Her voice in my head every time I can't sleep. Blues diffusing: 'I'm gonna sit right down and write myself a letter, and make believe it came from you . . .'

5

Begin with Chinnamastā, the sixth Mahāvidyā, she who cuts off her head to feed herself and her loved ones. I must destroy myself to feed myself; I must eat that which destroys me. My desire to feed my loved ones destroys me; my loved ones drink my blood. Hail Raktapānaparāyaṇā (she who is devoted to her own bloodthirst).

*

Manu said: 'A man who draws blood will be eaten by others in the next world for as many years as the number of dust particles from the earth that the spilled blood lumps together.'

*

Begin with spilled blood, with rain breaking up lumps of dust and blood, with rain dissolving the sacrificial site, the image of devotion and destruction. Begin with the dust from her feet, rain washing away the traces of whereabouts, the traces of body, the traces of metaphor; begin without blood, without dirt, begin with symbolic emaciation.

2

'Is she anywhere after this, is she too far for us?'

स्फोट sphoṭa,

m. bursting, opening, expansion, disclosure; extension; a swelling, boil, tumour; a little bit or fragment, chip; crackling, crash, roar; (in philosophy) sound (conceived as eternal, indivisible, and creative); the eternal and imperceptible element of sounds and words and the real vehicle of the idea which bursts or flashes on the mind when a sound is uttered

स्फोटा sphoṭā,

f. shaking or waving the arms

In the Rainstorm

In 1755, lexicographer Samuel Johnson made his great attempt to 'fix' or 'embalm' the English language. Sometime during his decade-long labour, he realised the impossibility of the task, as he recalls in the preface to *A Dictionary of the English Language*:

> Total and sudden transformations of a language seldom happen; conquests and migrations are now very rare; but there are other causes of change, which, though slow in their operation, and invisible in their progress, are perhaps as much superior to human resistance, as the revolutions of the sky, or intumescence of the tide.

His comments were prescient. Thirty years after his dictionary was published, a cataclysm broke upon the English language.

Johnson believed that English was primarily derived from Roman and Teutonic languages, but in 1786, philologer Sir William Jones discovered that the branches extended much further. He proposed that ancient Greek, Latin, Sanskrit, Persian, Gothic and Celtic languages shared a linguistic source, and what is now known as the Indo-European language family began to take root. 'Oriental' or 'Selim' Jones, as he was nicknamed, extended the study to include the religions associated with these ancient and classical languages. Distant cultures became comparable as linguistic and mythological distinctions were swept by tides; East and West were not as disparate as supposed. (Two hundred and fifty years after the discovery, this secret remains guarded by philological lexicon and decompression sickness.)

By placing Dyauṣ [*pitṛ*], Zeus [*pater*] and Jupiter alongside one another, Jones discovered the multiplicity of the Sky-Father. And the whole earth was of one language. Are Abraham and Sarah versions of Brahmā and Sarasvatī? Is Zeus Isis Jesus Kṛṣṇa Christ?

> This is not intended as casting a slur on Sir W. Jones. At his time the principles which have now been established by the

students of the science of language were not yet known, and as with words, so with the names of deities, similarity of sound, the most treacherous of all sirens, was the only guide in such researches.

I began the study of Sanskrit after a friend told me that this ancient language is poetry itself. Imagine the correct words breaking loose, line breaks arranging themselves in the burble. The terms of the promise are manifest: Sanskrit, *saṃ-skṛta*, well-formed, perfection, of the gods, the beauty of artifice; hallowing convention, preserving numbers, names of rivers and the rounded shapes of the aftersound. I am not alone in the *sanctum sanctorum*, nor free from intrusion. The nineteenth-century lexicographer Sir Monier Monier-Williams, author of a Sanskrit-English dictionary, guides me through the language like poetry; I crouch in definitions, dragging lamps.

Monier-Williams's Sanskrit-English dictionary was first published in Oxford in 1899. This immense lexicographical project – 'dry, dreary and thankless drudgery' as he described it, alluding to Johnson – was undertaken in his capacity as Boden Professor of Sanskrit at the University of Oxford. This position was funded by Colonel Boden, who stated in his will that 'the special object of his munificent bequest was to promote the translation of the Scriptures into Sanskrit, so as "to enable his countrymen to proceed in the conversion of the natives of India to the Christian Religion."' Monier-Williams respectfully included this quotation in his preface to the dictionary.

In 1860, a ruthless campaign for the professorship took place in British newspapers and captured public interest. Max Müller, the defeated rival, was the superior linguist, but he had never set foot in India, he was German, and he held liberal Christian views. This last characteristic proved to be the least forgivable. Monier-Williams was a devout evangelist and unequivocal in his approach:

> But what we assert is, that the national character is cast in a
> Sanskrit mould, and that the Sanskrit language and literature
> is not only the key to a vast and apparently confused and

unmeaning religious system, but it is also the one medium of approach to the hearts of the Hindus, however unlearned, or however disunited by the various circumstances of country, caste, and creed. It is, in truth, even more to India than classical and patristic literature was to Europe at the time of the Reformation. It gives a deeper impress to the Hindu mind than the latter ever did to the European; so that a missionary at home in Sanskrit will be at home in every corner of our vast Indian territories.

Müller took a different view:

We all come from the East – all that we value most has come to us from the East, and in going to the East, not only those who have received a special Oriental training, but everybody who had enjoyed the advantages of a liberal, that is, of a truly historical education, ought to feel that he is going to his 'old home', full of memories, if only he can read them.

I am at home in a language that is not my own. When I work in Sanskrit, I lose myself in the dictionary's words; when I hear him speak, I forget the sound of my own voice. How could it be otherwise? I can only get to the language by means of the dictionary; Monier-Williams makes the connection, he whispers in my ear as Sanskrit speaks. This is my home, but he opens the door to let me in. My knowledge of Sanskrit will never exceed his; my love of Sanskrit will never be separate from him. I am not at home in this language although I should be, if *nomen est omen* is as heavy as it sounds. My name is Sanskrit, I ask Monier-Williams what I mean.

निशा **niśā**, f. night; a vision, dream; turmeric [Cf. *nak* & *nakti*; Zd. *nakht-uru*, *nakht-ru*; Gk. **νύξ**; Lat. *nox*; Lith. *naktis*; Slav. *nošti*; Goth. *nahts*; Angl. Sax. *neaht*, *niht*, Engl. night, Germ. *Nacht*.]

Listen closely, the one language speaks in scattered tongues.

Out of the Throat

Sanskrit was an oral language, meant to be passed between men, from Brahmin teacher to Brahmin student. Writing came late to Sanskrit; Brahmi, the first known South Asian script, is dated to circa 250 BCE. There were concerns about the democratisation of Sanskrit, as writing made the language accessible to women and lower castes. Linguistic historian Sheldon Pollock describes the ideology of orality:

> Long after writing became an everyday practice in the Sanskrit world, a bias toward the oral persisted; knowledge that is *kaṇṭhastha*, 'in the throat,' or memorized, was invariably privileged over knowledge that is *granthastha*, 'in a book.' Moreover, the representation of knowledge (or understanding or awareness) itself as impregnated by language-as-speech – and never language-as-text – radically differentiates the medieval Indian world from Latinate Europe of the same epoch.

But Sanskrit did not deteriorate on contact with paper, it remains in all of its qualities (*sarvaguṇa*, every single thread, every string of every musical instrument, the merit of a total composition, endowed with every excellence, valid through all parts). Sanskrit is usually written in Devanāgarī, but there is no attachment to any script in particular, so people can read and write Sanskrit in letters of their choosing. The one language writes in multiple hands. Transliteration is no crime; promise to sound it out one syllable at a time and you will walk out of the divine-city-writing unpunished. My first teacher (an Irish woman with her own pronunciation of mantras) said something like: 'It doesn't matter if you don't know what the words mean, they know you and speak you clearly.'

Little Mothers

अ **a** unreality

ऋ **ṛ** destroying

ए **e** sandalwood

आ **ā** smelling

ॠ **ṝ** destroying

ऐ **ai** vacuity

इ **i** clean knowledge

ऌ **ḷ** power

ओ **o** wind

अं **aṃ** shapes

अः **aḥ** the hand

क **ka** power

च **ca** unreality

ट **ṭa** hearing

त **ta** skin

प **pa** inner part

ख **kha** always kind

छ **cha** any fine art

ठ **ṭha** ready wit

थ **tha** the eye

फ **pha** protector

ग **ga** able to do

ज **ja** self-consciousness

ड **ḍa** self-consciousness

द **da** organ of taste

ब **ba** the hand

य **ya** touching

र **ra** shapes

ल **la** melted butter

श **śa** vacuity

ष **ṣa** wind

स **sa** fire

ह **ha** any fluid

ई **ī** destroying   उ **u** power   ऊ **ū** power

औ **au** the sharp edge

घ **gha** clean knowledge ङ **ṅa** great unreality
झ **jha** nature ञ **ña** soul or spirit
ढ **ḍha** mind ण **ṇ** hearing
ध **dha** smelling न **n** speech
भ **bha** foot म **m** cry aloud

व **va** fixed order

The Lexicographer-Priest

myths are distributed
authored by atmosphere
the goddess disappears underground

how unexpected
to attend to the satellite
yad ihāsti tad anyatra yan nehāsti na tat kvacit
('what is here is there; what is not here is nowhere')

the river is tangled in nomenclature
Prakṛti, Sarasvatī, Vāc blowing out of course
subject to the curves of the shell

boundless and destitute
characterised by daring
her body contradicts the definition

coated in white petals, tide-bound
she awaits the synonymous burst

presume the sea, presume the swell
the force of documentary proof

defined by putting together
bringing in close connection
nāmnāmmālā, string of beads, lexicon

words are lotus flowers looped on a wreath
the familiarity of the image cocoons
soft cups possessed by the line
uphold the agreement made to caprice

he makes boxes and sheaths for seed-vessels
syllables bloom and smile
liberated by dark corners

these are monuments to fragility
in an ambiguous resting ground
words show through the page where they should not

one surpasses pearls
the other dances

there was no death in the family
expiations went unperformed
the river deemed redundant

see who stands in front of you
see who was never there
lines drawn in shadow
passages undercut

etymology is placing white crowns on confluence

> It is remarkable that, in reviewing my collection, I found the
> word SEA unexemplified.

अपार **apāra**, not having an opposite shore
(the prefix 'a' negates the beyond)

अपारपार **apārapāra**, that which will not acquiesce

तरंग **taraṃga**, 'across-goer', a wave, billow

तरंगमालिन् **taraṃgamālin**, the sea as garlanded by waves

बन्ध **bandha**, binding, fixing, bandage, chain
there is no use conferring

मध्य **madhya**, used like *medius*
earth as a woman's body, the sea as her waist

रत्ननिधि **ratnanidhi**, the place where pearls are kept

this vessel is the final resting place
before the ocean churns

> If the changes that we fear be thus irresistible, what remains
> but to acquiesce with silence, as in the other insurmountable
> distresses of humanity? It remains that we retard what we
> cannot repel, that we palliate what we cannot cure. Life may
> be lengthened by care, though death cannot be ultimately
> defeated: tongues, like governments, have a natural tendency
> to degeneration; we have long preserved our constitution, let us
> make some struggles for our language.

महीप **mahīpa**, 'earth-protector'
conversant with words, compiling defeat and invention

the lexicographer exhales
grasping the fix as it blossoms

so many things lost in the deluge
how strangely they hold up in light

Notes on Sanskrit

Commentary on *Śrī Devī Uvāca* [The Great Goddess Said]
'It was all the difference between a chaos and a kosmos, between
the blind play of chance and an intelligible and therefore an
intelligent providence. How many souls, even now, when
everything else has failed them, when they have parted with the
most cherished convictions of their childhood, when their faith
in man has been poisoned, and when the apparent triumph of all
that is selfish, ignoble, and hideous, has made them throw up the
cause of truth, of righteousness, and innocence as no longer worth
fighting for, at least in this world; how many, I say, have found their
last peace and comfort in the contemplation of the *ṛta*, of the order
of the world, whether manifested in the unvarying movement of
the stars, or revealed in the unvarying number of the petals, and
stamens, and pistils of the smallest forgot-me-not!'

The laws of this language reflect the laws of the universe, we
might never come closer to truth. This language does things to
me, this language that speaks you more than you know. This is
me putting you into practice. The linguistic and grammatical
sequence parallels spiritual progression.

Mātṛkā [Alphabet]
It bears repeating: the body of the goddess, divided into lots of little
mothers. Everyone must receive the allotted part:

'It is in this sense that the universe is said to be composed of the
letters. It is the fifty (or as some count them fifty-one) letters of
the Sanskrit alphabet which are denoted by the Garland of severed
heads which the naked Mother Kālī, dark like a threatening
rain-cloud, wears as She stands amidst bones and carrion, beasts
and birds, in the burning ground, on the white corpse-like body
of Śiva. For it is She who 'slaughters', that is, withdraws all speech

and its objects into Herself at the time of the dissolution of all things (*Mahāpralaya*).'

Vowels are organised in order of transcendence, consonants in order of manifestation. Categories of letters are categories of existence: voiceless and voiced, unaspirated and aspirated. Mothers position themselves accordingly, from the back of the throat to the palate to the alveolar ridge to the teeth to the lips. Mothers are talking amongst themselves or they are worried about you or they are doing their best to protect you – you weren't put on this world to speak for yourself.

Pada [Word]
Sometimes it seems like every word is another word for an astrological measurement (what are lunar mansions anyway) or a species of fig tree or the opposite of the action or one of the four stages of something or the *pudendum muliebre*. ('Pudenda' are 'the shameful parts'; 'muliebrity' is womanhood, as opposed to virility, chiefly obsolete [OED] – Monier-Williams can be so delicate!)

Vyākaraṇa [Grammar]
'Grammar is . . . the door of freedom, the medicine for the diseases of language, the purifier of all sciences; it sheds its light on them; . . . it is the first rung on the ladder that leads up to realisation of supernatural powers, and the straight royal road for those who seek freedom.'

You have entered the teacher's house.

Liṅga [Gender]
Holding on to its gender; having the gender of another; an absence of gender; having a gender that agrees; having a fixed gender; an impotent gender; a gender like a cloud without water; a gender like a lotus leaf; a third nature gender; a twofold gender; destitute of both genders; having the mark of a gender; the incongruity of gender; a gender that prevents old age and prolongs life; gender as a remedy for magical purposes; gender doubtful;

variegating gender; gender in the image of god; gender that has an origin and is therefore liable to be destroyed; a change of gender; the laws of gender; gender unknown; gender as a kind of ornament; gender as the meaning of words; another gender is required; having a gender that shares in everything; preserving its gender; gender of doubtful derivation that applies to closely connected things.

Vākya [Sentence]
'With streaming clouds trumpeting like haughty tuskers,
with lightning-banners and drum beats of thunder claps,
in towering majesty, the season of rains
welcome to lovers, now comes like a king, my love.'

'Western wind, when will thou blow,
The small rain down can rain?
Christ, if my love were in my arms
And I in my bed again!'

'Yet there are subtler clouds, all the tenuous shadows of swift and uncertain source which pass across the relationship, changing its light and its modeling; suddenly it is another landscape, a faint black intoxication. The cloud, then, is no more than this: *I'm missing something.*'

Sādhanā [Practice]
'[Ritual] is an activity governed by explicit rules. The important thing is what you do, not what you think, believe or say. In India this has become a basic feature of all religion, so that we should refer, not to the faithful or orthodox, but to the orthoprax (from Greek *orthos*, "right" and *praxis*, "action").'

Mantra [Sacred Formula]
The pleasure of syllables like so many pearl ornaments in the Hyderabadi style. In this context, we can say with confidence: form is sometimes more than an extension of content: 'Mantras

are a typical product of Indian civilisation – a civilisation where form is all-important.'

Cit [Consciousness]
Everything can be compared to the belly of a fish (the puffing and sucking of subjectivity, space, time), an image that makes me squeamish. You are more powerful when her belly protrudes, it means the sacrifices are well received.

Parāvāc [The Supreme Voice]
Abhinavagupta said: 'In that stage, there is absolutely no thought of difference such as "this" (a particular entity or individual), "thus" (a particular form), "here" (particular space), "now" (particular time).' In all seriousness, she is the most perfect container.

Samādhi [Union]
He hires a pilot to write 'unity in multiplicity' and 'diversity in unity' in the sky and asks her to accept whichever one she likes best. She reads *Tender Buttons* with her friends and they make each other feel uncomfortable and repel new friends. They sit in the garden hoping her lavender-attachment doesn't become a eucalyptus-sized problem. She looks at postcards of nuns and witches and decides it's time to put the psychoanalysis away.

Samāsa [Compound]
Love / the sound between them / the bit of a bridle; firmness / the sound between them / the bit of a bridle; fragrance / the sound between them / the bit of a bridle, and so on. Child of different of child; her debt of debt her; she serves all sorts of misfortune of sorts all serves she, and so on.

Notes on Tantra

Tantra may be understood as the knowledge that spreads. Many Hindu beliefs and practices can be traced to Tantric origins, such as yoga, mantra, *mudrā*, the *cakra* system, the use of sacred diagrams and the role of the guru. At the same time, Tantra is felt to be the dark and dangerous underside of Hinduism. Tantra may or may not comprise:

- pre-Aryan religious traditions circa 2500–1750 BCE (this hypothesis finds evidence in terracotta artefacts – particularly feminine figurines – found in excavations of the Indus Valley);
- multiple texts emerging from Hindu, Buddhist and Jain cultures circa 600–1700 CE (this timespan includes several Tantric revivals or renaissances);
- and continuing Indigenous traditions of village deities and unorthodox ritual practices, often contrasted with Aryan, Sanskrit and Vedic cultures (which emphasise masculine gods and caste-based hierarchies).

Tantra is marked by its difficulty by devotees, practitioners and scholars; I am drawn to its experiments, oddities and contradictions. Despite slipping into mainstream South Asian and Western cultures (yoga, New Age spirituality, Tantric sex), Tantra remains emphatically different. Hugh B. Urban describes the extremity of Tantra in terms of its 'radical Otherness, the fact that it is considered to be the most radical aspect of Indian spirituality, the one most diametrically opposed to the modern West.' He argues that 'Tantra [is] singled out as India's darkest, most irrational element – as the Extreme Orient, the most exotic aspect of the exotic Orient itself.' Any attempt to comprehend Tantra is made problematic by its resistance to definition.

तन् tan, v. to extend, spread, be diffused (as light) over, shine, extend towards, reach to; to continue, endure; to stretch (a cord), extend or bend (a bow), spread, spin out, weave; to prepare (a way for); to direct (one's way) towards; to (spread i.e.) speak (words); to put forth, show, manifest, display; to accomplish, perform (a ceremony); to sacrifice; to compose (a literary work)

तन्त्र tantra, n. a loom; the warp; the leading or principal or essential part, system, framework; doctrine, rule, theory, chapter of such a work; a class of works teaching magical and mystical formularies (mostly in the form of dialogues between Śiva and Durgā and said to treat of five subjects: 1. the creation, 2. the destruction of the world, 3. the worship of the gods, 4. the attainment of all objects, esp. of six superhuman faculties, 5. the four modes of union with the supreme spirit by meditation); a spell; oath or ordeal; a means which leads to two or more results, contrivance; chief remedy; happiness

तन्त्री tantrī, f. the wire or string of a lute; (figuratively) the strings of the heart; any tubular vessel of the body, sinew, vein; a girl with peculiar qualities; name of a river

Tantra is the practice of extending, of stretching to make connections, of creating something from those connections. Tantra is the weaving of multiple threads and the extrication of one part from the whole. Tantra is literal, metaphorical and abstract; historic, mythic and imaginary; formal, ethical and philosophical. Tantra spins and loops, challenging categories, making you forget which route you took to get here, why you came and how you feel about it all. Tantra is a sacrifice, a poem, a spell, a song – the plucks and glides of your body as you bend between what you want and what you are able to do or to have.

The weave suggests other mythologies. There is Theseus, the labyrinth and the ball of string; Arachne's transformation into a spider; the Lady of Shalott and her mirror work. A few years ago, someone told me about the Navaho tradition of the spirit line, and I made the following notes: 'He says things like: "My right brain is a wild stallion; my left brain is a kitten." He talks about the "spirit-line" in Native textiles, the flaw in the pattern through which you are able to escape, like the earth wire for your soul. He talks about being the "singer and the song; the poet and the poem". I feel embarrassed by his methodology, I struggle to explain my own, and this record of our conversation reaches to touch me.

Ritual Steps for a Tantric Poetics

this is the way to north
the honey love of air
poetry and myth lick your ears
this is the way to northeast
the drunk eyes of air-fire
forgetting you slip into dialect
this is the way to east
the hurting hold of fire
your tongue becomes strange to you
this is the way to southeast
the sad smoke of fire-water
soak your loneliness in cold water
this is the way to south
the blood sacrifice of water
dance on their backs as they copulate
this is the way to southwest
the inner heat of water-earth
knowledge cauterizes
this is the way to west
the earth body of earth
write the flash before subjectivity
this is the way to northwest
the three points of earth-air
consider geometrical process
this is the way to above
the safe crossing of above
etymology as your ladder
this is the way to below
the dead time of below
your fear the words mean nothing

come away from north
assume the contemporary
you have access to more words than you are using
come away from northeast
try on as many voices as you like
impressions imply re-making
come away from east
your bones, your blood vessels, your eyelashes
how astonishing, astonishing
come away from southeast
the confessional sounds you make in the bath
you are so much more than feeling
come away from south
the obscure narratives you rely on
start again with blood and iron
come away from southwest
your arms are scarred with procedure
you were wrong about sealed containers
come away from west
before essentialism smothers you
get out, get out, get out
come away from northwest
the constraints you have reasoned yourself into
stare at flowers until something happens
come away from above
the warmth of academic contexts
unless you can sweat it out
come away from below
extending words to the breaking
the charm has wound down

Correspondence as Writing System

Correspondence is a garland of skulls that may be divided absolutely into 1 or 2 or 3 or 4 or 10 or 50 or 51 or 108 or 1000 or 1008 skulls. This calculation is correct, repeatedly, to the point of vivisection.

For example, a mother as not less than measure as not less than authority as not less than light as not less than knowledge as not less than binding; fettering as not less than death as not less than a woman's waist.

This example is untimely, and stubbornly so; lazy returns painted on handicraft paper. Following pseudo-Vedic manuscripts, we apologise ourselves into disarticulation.

Survival disables the open mind.

We circulate stars: a dark blue transit, a counterfeit ring, a rose bush grows beneath the table.

Obstructed by the space that is saving for you, my interior distends: the first to the first, the blood to the blood, the divesting of colourless fields.

She is afflicted by this geological era insofar as her activities are the colour of spoiled meat. But the generally felt precedes the disgrace of seasoning.

Home is a collection of contagious objects.

She licks the lid of the project.

Correspondence as Make Believe

Consider this divinely ordained climax of history and the filthy soles of her feet. She has been walking around corners, running together in afterthoughts, disambiguating like rain.

One hand on my shoulder, the other pointing to a London parakeet, she says: 'You never seemed to be waiting.'

Underestimating the logistics, I sit down in the middle of the path.

The break anticipates the arrangement, as long as the hands continue to shake.

You raise your arms, as if we were sleeping together, as if the suspension came as a surprise.

Ever-making is a series of shades: the sun in your face, will you get that fair sun out of my face.

The parakeet is a divinely ordained climax of history, which is always out of place.

She catches honeybees in her hair and green feathers in her teeth.

Make Believe as Sacrifice

Taking a position before making an attack, the shares you have accrued change colour; you miscalculate which parts of yourself it is OK to waste.

One hand points to the solar path, the other points beneath the table.

You must crawl through broken mirrors and perfectly weighted steak knives. You must talk under the dismemberment of the project, sludging your cuts with commitment:

may the season not surpass you	[*mā kālas tvām aty-agāt*]
may the improper not surpass you	[*mā kālas tvām aty-agāt*]
may the enemy not surpass you	[*mā kālas tvām aty-agāt*]
may the dying not surpass you	[*mā kālas tvām aty-agāt*]
may the meat not surpass you	[*mā kālas tvām aty-agāt*]
may the waiting not surpass you	[*mā kālas tvām aty-agāt*]
may the perceptible not surpass you	[*mā kālas tvām aty-agāt*]
may the fixed points not surpass you	[*mā kālas tvām aty-agāt*]
may the dark blue not surpass you	[*mā kālas tvām aty-agāt*]
may the devouring not surpass you	[*mā kālas tvām aty-agāt*]

Correspondence is make believe is sacrifice is practising a falling exchange: Which parts of yourself to which soft curses?

Spreading is saving is practising which parts to save?

Her Voice as an Instrument of Thought

The verbal root of 'mantra' is *man*, to think, believe, imagine (cognate with ancient Greek μένω, *méno̱*, to stay or endure, μέμονα, *mémona*, to wish or intend; Latin *meminisse*, to remember or bear in mind, *monere*, to remind or instruct or teach; and English 'to mean'). André Padoux explains that the suffix *-tra* is used to construct words denoting instruments and objects, and may connote the verb *trai*, to protect, preserve, rescue. In *Vāc: The Concept of the Word in Selected Hindu Tantras*, he writes:

> Mantras are always regarded as a form of speech differing from language in that, unlike language, they are not bound by 'conventions' nor associated with objects, but on the contrary are oriented toward the very origin of the Word and of the energy.

The Word, in this context, is Vāc, the goddess of voice, speech, language and sound, or the philosophical concept thereof.

The most powerful and prevalent mantra in Hinduism is *om* or *aum*. *Om* has many names: the immoveable, unchangeable mantra; the outpouring heart mantra; the self-existent, absolute mantra; the sap and taste of anything mantra; the womb of knowledge mantra; the form of knowledge mantra; the substance of knowledge mantra; the repeated truth mantra; the eternally sounding mantra; the omniscient mantra; the binding, bordering mantra; the roaring, bellowing mantra. *Om* is categorised as a *bīja* mantra. *Bīja* is seed, germ, element, primary cause or source. *Bīja* mantras are monosyllabic mantras considered to be sound without meaning; they have no etymological root and no semantic value.

In *Ritual and Mantras: Rules Without Meaning*, Frits Staal argues that the *bīja* mantra is a remnant of prehistoric culture that has more in common with birdsong than it does with language:

> It seems likely that human language is not as old as was once believed: perhaps around one hundred thousand years . . .

Ritual is much older; Neanderthaler man had elaborate rituals . . . This is supported by the facts of animal ritualization which are similar to human rituals especially with regard to their structure . . . It is likely that the same holds for mantras, for mantras occupy a domain that is situated between ritual and language.

He speculates that if mantra is older than language, perhaps a similar phenomenon may be found in animal behaviour. After considering the syntax, usage and ritualization of bird song, Staal concludes:

The similarity between mantras and bird songs is due not to common function, but to common non-functionality. Mantras and bird songs share not only certain structural properties, but also lack of an inherent or absolute purpose. It is precisely these features that express the common characteristic of both as essentially satisfying, pleasurable and playful – features that, in the case of mantras, have remained even though language has intervened.

Such an interpretation may not be welcomed by Tantric devotees, who are all too familiar with assessments of mantra as 'meaningless jabber' or 'gibberish', to repeat Sir John Woodroffe's anecdote. (Woodroffe was an early twentieth century judge and scholar of British-Indian law who lived a double life as Arthur Avalon, Tantric devotee, publishing many writings on the subject.) He repudiates:

Though a Mantra such as a *Bīja*-mantra may not convey its meaning on its face, the initiate knows that its meaning is the own form (*Svarūpa*) or the particular *Devatā* [deity] whose Mantra it is, and the essence of the *Bīja* is that which makes letters sound, and exists in all which we say or hear. Every Mantra is thus a particular sound form (*Rūpa*) of the *Brahman* [Supreme Being].

Returning to the definition of *bīja* as seed or source; remembering that *vāc* refers to human and animal languages (and to the sounds of inanimate objects, such as the stones used for pressing); fixing the mind on the embodiments of mantra, the Mahāvidyās (who are associated with crows, cranes and green parrots) . . . I wonder if this talk of meaning is really about something else.

Vāc is the mother of the Vedas, the mother of knowledge, the cow who feeds the world. She is chopped in four directions.

Sacrifice walks in her footsteps, begging forgiveness for the murders of her mothers and fathers, asking her if she would like anything else. Priests hurry after, trying to remember the order in which it all happened. They wrap the remains in loose sections of their cotton sets.

(We must thank the priests for their seeing and their stories, for they became mad with knowing. We must thank the students for their ordering and their poetry, for they became mad without knowing.)

The rivers are formed of poetic metres and the metres udders and the feathers voice; as Arthur Avalon said: 'The recitation of a Mantra without knowing its meaning is practically fruitless. I say "practically" because devotion, even though it be ignorant, is never wholly void of fruit.'

Two birds sit at the top of a fig tree. One eats while the other watches.

They prayed to the cow and drained her vigour. There were floods in heaven: before as a warning, or during in sympathy, or after to signal the new regime.

Vedic priests were keen to separate their voices from the voices of the people. They gave one quarter of Vāc to humankind for speech, they concealed the rest for their own purposes. The people spoke for hundreds of years, not realising how much more voice could be. Eventually Tantric priests appeared on the scene, eager to dismantle borders and make spiritual information available to all (with the exception of Tantric secrets, which most people couldn't handle anyway). They elucidated the four stages of *vāc*:

वैखरी vaikharī, f. speech in the fourth of its four stages from the first stirring of the air or breath, articulate utterance, that utterance of sounds or words which is complete as consisting of full and intelligible sentences. This is the gross level, this is speech for bodies and for differentiation. These are words with hard faces that you don't want to look at in case you hear too much

मध्यमा madhyamā, f. the womb. The intermediate level, between the gross and the subtle. Language moves further away from activity. There are signs, although you cannot see them, that the garland is arranging itself. If you want to do poetry, do it now. The lights in your house shine blue

पश्यन्ती paśyantī, f. a harlot. She is known as 'the Visionary'. Your body bleeds objectivity, she must be getting close. Abhinavagupta said: 'Therefore, *paśyantī* comprehends in a general indeterminate way whatever is desired to be known if it is awakened by due causal conditions just as one who has experienced variegated colour like dark, blue, etc., as in a peacock's tail and whose experience is determined by many impressions, positive and negative, recalls only that particular colour which is awakened by the proper causal condition of memory.'

परावाच् parāvāc, f. the supreme voice. She is the anti-unconscious, the anti-dark. She contains every word, every action, every object and every share of the sacrifice. She combines the four stages in her supreme silence; as Abhinavagupta said: 'This non-answer or silence is the highest truth.' She is the relentless throbbing of 'I am' (*aham*), the all-voice in the all-head, which suddenly becomes all-quiet when you ask a question and demonstrate your willingness to listen

These stages of voice, speech, language and sound correspond to stages of knowledge, belief and practice, which may be understood as a key.

Padoux notes with an exclamation mark that *vāc* is a feminine word. I return to etymology in irritation at his surprise.

Mantra, from *man*, derived from the Proto-Indo-European root **men*, which offers three tempting branches: to think, to stay, to stand. The first leads us to the Roman goddess Minerva, grave goddess of wisdom and the arts. The second to the ancient Greek Mnemosyne, or Memory, mother of the muses, the goddesses of poetic inspiration. The third to the Hindu mountain Mandara, used by the gods and demons as a churning stick to recover the nectar of immortality and the lotus-flower goddess. Or to the Hindu mountain Kailāśa, the abode of Śiva and Pārvatī, which holds the lake Mānasa ('belonging to mind or spirit').

To complete the cycle, I will mention that Pārvatī's name means mountain and that she is an *avatāra* of Vāc. But now I am annoyed at myself and these lengths and this rendering of proof. Does she speak? Does she write? What is the matter of myth? What use if the answer is unintelligible? What use if the answer is no?

Correspondence as a Compass on the Body

The capitalised pronoun is a misdirection; I head for the kingdom round the corners of your untucked shirt.

Your arms are the limit of darkness and light, encircling the world and that which is not the world.

How else can I say this?

I feel myself decomposing in your thin arms.

The gloit struggles to describe itself, delaying the performance of its duty.

Determining my daily revolutions, you send me in circles, as a line returns to itself.

We are dispossessed by the knowledge of each other's address. Or, it's disorienting to know where you are.

The slub invites you to look.

Asserting its interest, the slub confirms the invitation.

We joke about social dissolution in the same place, at different times, which you hear as consonance, but I don't like the way I sound in your mouth.

What do you say?

The composition of the room discloses the rendering of the search.

You tidy to signal the end of the party, or, the world is topsy-turvy because you are looking for love.

Thirteen Days after Death
(18–30 April 2015)

The First Day

The first day is the day that she died.

It was a bad time to die, according to the astrological charts, and in the days that followed we assumed the responsibility for her delivery. I use 'delivery' in place of the Sanskrit word *mokṣa*. *Mokṣa* is release, such as the liberation of an eclipsed planet, or the untying of hair, or the settling of a question.

Do you think you will change your plans?

Now that she is gone, do you think you will come back?

Relatives, friends and neighbours visit on a daily basis. One after another they remember her: the beautiful saris that she wore to kitty parties, the fried eggs that she sent down to the nursing home.

They remember her dancing; I imagine a version of my grandmother who could dance.

No one can determine this ultimate release, the consequences of soul once departed from body, but the family can ensure the integrity of the departure itself.

Her father was bad news from a noble family. Her mother died when she was still too young to remember. She must have been beautiful, otherwise he wouldn't have married her; she must have been good, otherwise she wouldn't have disappeared.

We hear stories of deer and peacocks roaming the palace grounds, of white tigers and open-top cars. Of an African grey parrot in a golden cage, drinking teaspoons of whisky and answering the phone. Of her never feeling at home in her childhood home.

On the sixth day, we drive towards Nagarjuna Sagar Dam; the bones must be deposited in a confluence. We step into a coracle on the right bank and the boatman steers us to some rocks in the middle of the waters. He issues instructions: repeat *nārāyaṇa* three times, smash the earthenware pot against the rocks, toss the bones into the water behind you, and don't look back!

Viṣṇu said: 'Fondly attached to their sons, wives and relations, men sink in the ocean of worldliness, as old and worn out wild elephants are drowned in one and the same ocean through an unconquerable instinct of companionship.'

Kṛṣṇa said: 'Your words are wise, Arjuna, but your sorrow is for nothing. The truly wise mourn neither for the living nor for the dead. There was never a time when I did not exist, nor you, nor any of these kings. Nor is there any future in which we shall cease to be.'

Our home has always depended on the fact of her presence and her protection. We are responsible for the surrender and enunciation of her delivery.

84

I sit on the floor in her bedroom, pulling plastic bags, biscuit tins and newspaper-wrapped bundles out of her wardrobes. I am urgent to discover her.

The X-rays of her knee replacements and the heave of her walk.

A grandchild's drawing of a magic carpet with a speech bubble.

A snakeskin purse, reminding her boys of the marble floor, the cobra as it passed over the backs of their necks, and jasmine and marigold garlands.

His first wife's silver bangle, and all of those people who left the ends of their lives to her.

An envelope filled with illustrations of Gaṇeśa cut out of greetings cards and wedding invitations, a cross-stitch embroidery of a swan, Telugu translations, other unfinished projects.

The passport that expired the year she stopped walking.

I always thought that she preferred Hanumān, because of his relationship to Rāma, but she developed an aversion to monkeys in her last few years.

I had hoped that you would meet her.

She made the requisite daily sacrifices – worship, hospitality and charity – and I realise the source of our extravagances, as a river is purified by its current.

She loved diving and swimming and posing for photographs with wicker baskets and curved swords.

She begins to tell the story of how they first met: 'I was closing the door and dancing in the room. They climbed up and seen me how I danced.' Pause to check her blood sugar levels. 'He came and saw me.' Her levels are high because she didn't have her tablets in the morning, and we will never know what he said when he saw her, or how she felt when she heard.

She displays photographs of deceased relatives in the house as a reminder that each forehead must be marked with red powder, that oil lamps and flowers must be placed before debts.

'The Simple Discharge of a Solemn Debt'

According to certain Hindu traditions, a person's afterlife is
determined by the observances of her family in the days and years
following her death. Whether the soul is bound for terrestrial
rebirth, temporary heavens and hells, or final release into the
Absolute and Eternal, its journey must be sustained by relatives
and descendants.

As a means of emotional and spiritual relief, the funeral is an
unlikely process. The incomprehensible depends upon yellow
jasmine and red roses, betel leaves and nuts, silver coins, cow
and bull figurines, coconuts, cooked rice and clarified butter.
Rearranging objects, images and presentations of grief, we help
each other into the punctiliousness and mess.

The crematorium is bordered with leaning slabs of white marble,
each inscribed with verses from the *Bhagavad Gītā*, the Song of God.

The unreal and untrue are not found,
There is no continuity of becoming.

There is continuity of becoming,
The true being and really existent are found,
As anyone or anything ought to be.

I force the Song of God to sound outside itself,
Struggling to find synonyms for God, or Supreme Being, or
Soul of the Universe.

We begin firmly, with intention and assent,
And are upended with a word that I cannot replace.

Fighting for all seeing and perception,
We are indestructible and utterly lost.

Efforts of self are exposed,
Definitions rendered ineffective by procedure.

The Song concludes with the last way,
Alike, devoted, and coming to nothing.

The procession halts three times on the way to the pyre. Abbé
Dubois said: 'Seeing that the spirits of the nether world or their
emissaries have been known to make mistakes in their choice and
to take one person for another, these halts are made to give plenty
of time for the spirits to recognize any mistakes they may have
made, so that no person may be thrown on the funeral pyre who
is still destined to live.' My uncle and father shake her shoulders,
tap her forehead and call her name, but she does not stir. The
procession continues.

Monier-Williams remarks that 'it is wholly inconsistent with
the true theory of Hinduism that the [funeral rites] should
deliver a man from the consequences of his own deeds. Manu
says, "Iniquity once practised, like a seed, fails not to yield its
fruit to him that wrought it"; but Hinduism bristles with such
inconsistencies.'

Affirmations of a world in all parts
Become irritants with each particle of prohibition and
negation.

According to the tone of voice, the standard line, 'she made
a career out of kindness', can be taken as a compliment or
an accusation. I think of her heart, 'the long parade to the
graveyard', Eurydice, how much of this is happening in reverse.

A subtlety that cannot be delegated, *mokṣa* rests between a soul
and its best binding knot.

How long do we wait? My father gestures with his hands: 'The skull must crack to allow the soul to escape.'

Vātamātmā

She is the centre around which we orientate.

She says that she feels breathless.

Does she complain of a vacuum in her heart, which seems dry, numbed, as if being broken?

The chain of weaving is the body I don't remember.

The lift reaches the second floor. Slide the grille, the first and second doors are already open. She is standing in the entrance, framed by the house.

Heart-knotted, relentless in failure.

Breath approaches blown, taking movement by force.

Has she carried heavy loads on the head, or laughed loudly, or talked loudly?

Walk into the house, turn right. The corridor leads to her bedroom, the door is open. She is sitting in the chair, positioned to greet you.

I set my weak heart upon weakness.

The promoter of speech we can't know I don't remember.

Always turn right. She is lying in bed, so if you don't walk into the bedroom, she won't know that you are there.

Spirit falls in the share of wind, leaving our bodies incoherent.

She says that she feels breathless.

The heart cannot fill with occasion, the full particulars of a narrative I don't remember.

Her great capacity for love, her sense of humour that falls on the right side of mischief.

Soul imparts air, the immediacy of our survival.

Glance down the corridor. She is sleeping and the door is almost closed. Sit and talk where she might hear you.

She says that she feels restless.

In the shorter half of the night, the winds which go everywhere.

Breathing again, taking heart again, for dancing and for laughter.

Our grief might be charted in the number of steps it takes to reach her.

Her always remembering you, and the little things that might make you happy.

States of the Body Produced by Love

स्मरदशा smaradaśā,

f. state of the body produced by love (ten states are named:
joy of the eyes, pensive reflection, desire, sleeplessness,
emaciation, indifference to external objects, abandonment
of shame, infatuation, fainting away, death)

Joy of the Eyes

On the future tense in Sanskrit: responses to the desire to arrive at the present by means of the past . . .

The future is not the beginning, but the forerunner, of a new intense formation.

The first time that you see me, you will see me, without implication of time.

The future expresses what is going to take place at some time to come, adding on the one hand an implication of will or intention, and on the other hand of promise or threatening.

If you, villain, had not stopped [*prāgrahīṣyaḥ*] my mouth, without any implication of time.

Circles of future and desiderative border one another; the one sometimes expected where the other might be met.

I, conditional, want you to stop my mouth; will you stop.

My mouth encircles the sustain of these refusals: sometimes and unexpected, unreasonable and polite.

If you, beautiful, would perceive this new stress formation, reducing the noise of our [*śyas*] tomorrow, heads shaved, future universe, 'victorious banners unlowered'.

Discipline of desire begins in the mouth.

Pensive Reflection

Imagine a time in which you feel happy. In your happiness, you imagine another time in which you feel unhappy. You are in bed, your love is in your arms; the room is cold and it belongs to you.

This is the tower of the past. The battlements are formed of anthills, the anthills the curves of the goddess, the curves snakes agreeing sealing themselves away. Lookouts lie face down, mouths open to the earth, swallowing the matter of their warnings. Lookouts are snakes.

In your unhappiness, you imagine another time in which you feel happy. You are standing, you catch sight of your love across the room. One or both of you is wearing a uniform. The room is warm; it does not belong to you.

The tower is oversaturated and impossible to date. Lookouts' mouths fill with earth, earth itching, itching converting warning to retch. Lookouts reduce the noise of their retching; snakes containing the warnings in the smoothed lines of their swallows.

This is how to conjugate the old future tense.

Desire

For the sake of standing, we would pull the warnings from the mouths of the lookouts.

We would pull out the tongues of our enemies.
We would paralyse.

The goddess, highly coloured, carries a knife.

You imagine her cutting tongues.
You would offer tongues.

[*yaje yakṣi yaṣṭāhe ca*] I sacrifice, I have sacrificed, and I shall sacrifice

The first tongue, the other (between two and infinity) tongues, the others speaking desire into desire.

You, paralysed, would let her into your mouth.
She would kiss your friends.

You, standing outside desire, would watch.

Sleeplessness

Past versions of you

Past versions of me dreaming past versions of you

Inherited dreams of you

Inherited qualities of me inherited from dreams of you

Inherited qualities of me you

Inherited qualities and strings of pearls and lightly wearing me you

Places where your pearls were lightly worn were like me unlikely you

Places where your loved ones were born you were born like-minded
     you me you

Places where your loved ones die in all likelihood you die you me you

Places where you'd die you would die your like-mindedness would
     die you you you

Singular moments of laughter you

Plural moments of laughter with you with you with you

Singular moments of fear of you of me of you

Plural moments of fear of walking with without these moments with
     you

Desiring to walk home to leave home to leave you

Desiring to leave home with you without you without you

Cleaning the room as if that's all you can do you

Cleaning the room cleaning and cleaning and missing you you

Squatting to clean and squatting and sitting and missing you me you

Unseating you are deep-seated within me you you you

Desiring to clean to unseat you to squat you
Desiring do not squat you do nothing you do nothing you
Images and actions are not images and actions you
Becoming visible ink on the walls of the mind you
Becoming characteristic of poetry you
Becoming sensibility of writers and readers of poetry you me you
Becoming visibility of the walls between minds you you you
Visibility of the walls is neither image nor action you me you
Shame at placing this moment beside that moment you me you
Shame at placing this room beside that room me me you

Retching between moments of laughter and fear you
Retching while walking not with you not like you
Retching the lengths between me and you me and you
Measuring lengths between wanting you having you
Measuring lengths between wanting having wanting having you you
    you
Finding ourselves in our friends they're like you they're you they're
    not like you
Finding ourselves on the outside we're inside we're like you we're
    not you
Finding ourselves wanting we're having we're not you we're
    not you
Inheriting your loved ones you are qualified by love you me you
Inheriting rooms I am further and further and further from you you
    you

Emaciation

The **य y** in Sanskrit stands in the closest relationship with the vowel **इ i** (short or long); the two exchange with one another in cases innumerable.

Learning our histories selectively, the lesson is corrupted and incorrectly applied:

> The yes in Sanskrit stands in the closest relationship with the I. The yes and the I exchange with one another in cases innumerable.

This is no optional interchange.

Very probably, the Sanskrit I has everywhere more of a yes-character than belongs to the corresponding European sound.

The yes is one of the most common of Sanskrit sounds.

This is how to conjugate our constitutional histories of yes. This is how to construct our constitutional identities around yes-sounds, yet, loyal, betrayal.

The flat of the tongue against the walls of the room. The reverberations of yes-sounds enforcing the I, the I, the I.

We yield to the hooks of these I-sounds, inside, history, independence.

The walls of the room blocking the sounds of the tongues on the hooks of the I.

Indifference to External Objects

NO POLICE THE GLORIOUS TALES OF we are taught not to see the difference OF YOUR GREATNESS when did you first see the difference VILLAGE NO GIRL PROTEST SEETHING we are taught to be proud of the difference DEATH GIRL DANCING NO ONE STOP THE when did you first feel proud NO IMPENDING NO ATTEMPTED concerned only with ourselves we must love ourselves VICTIM HONOURED concerned only with comparisons we must prefer ourselves we must be preferable DEMONSTRATED DEED WAS DONE love must be mutual the comparisons are insatiable PENALTY NAMED COMMON DEATH NO we desire to be loved by everybody DEATH ARRIVED NO we do not see everybody we desire their love BURNT ALIVE OR DOWRY EVEN NOW I TOOK THE we must be seen by the world what must be seen FORM OF KALI we are proud when did you first feel proud RULED OUT HONOUR NATION HEINOUS we are ashamed when did you first feel proud CAN EQUALITY OF KIND we are seen by the world when did you first feel proud DEVOTED WIFE BECOMES A we remember powerlessness enslaved by our power FEAR IS ARE SCALE EQUAL SCARE WE our dirty habits our shamelessness our fatalism STEM THE ROT ALLOWING we are capable of love we love our families UNENDURABLE OF OUR SOCIETY we are capable of shame we are ashamed of our families NO IS POWER we are ashamed of our homes we are proud of our homes MURDER THE IDEAL we are brought up to welcome you into our homes BODY NOT YET SHADOW CHATTEL I am brought up to say yes to you ORAL NAKED BODY LEGAL SPIRIT OF THE GIRL I am brought up to be closed in my family I am brought up to be open at home FORCING FAILED TO SET ABLAZE my family is proud of me BOYS POTENTIAL TREATING ROWDIES GENDER YOGIC FLAMES my family is proud of me I would break my arms to defend my family IMMOLATED BODY IN THEM SUBSIDIES NO SHAME I am alone at home I arm myself to break my family CHARGES WHO SUSTAINED I undo my upbringing I am alone at home BETTER IF YOU DON'T I must shave my head to sustain my aloneness EVEN NAMES OF SEXUAL FIRE EXPRESSING GRIEF I lose my hair I am shameless at home SEXUAL DEATH WOULD DEATH OPPOSE how you love something and need nothing DEMON POWER PUNISH GODDESS how you love nothing and need something OUT CAME KALI FROM HER FOREHEAD how you love something and feel unhappy SAFETY BRUTAL BLAME POLICE COMES how you love nothing and feel unhappy NO AMEND OF HOME SUCH CASES EFFORTS WOULD OFFENCE how you need something and feel unhappy GOVERNMENT SHE TURNED UPON HER how you need nothing and feel unhappy FATHER YOU ARE VAIN AND WICKED how you begin with shame as if shame were the beginning NOW ASHAMED TO CALL MYSELF YOUR how you end with shame as if shame were the ending I WILL CAST MY WORTHLESS BODY how you withdraw from pride HONOUR VICTIM MARRY ONLY CONQUER ME IN how you withdraw from desire BATTLE HUMBLE AND MY PRIDE how you withdraw from gratitude AND THE SHAMEFUL DEEDS PRETENDED TO AFRAID ALAS SPARE how you withdraw from consent I AM HELPLESS yes what is it yes what do you want yes indeed yes is it so

Abandonment of Shame

The structure and process of abandonment of shame involves śleṣa, *or simultaneous narrative, ambiguity, clinging sexual disunion. There is a movement from shame to abandon, which looks like a human body, predetermined by* bhūdevas *[gods on earth], bonded by sacred duties of debt, untying white threads and uncovering itself. The naked body squats and struggles with knots, uncoils and loosens fine hair. The body sounds like hum, utterance, exclamation, expelling duty by reverberations of force. Gods and goddesses blossom and are annihilated. There is a movement from self-sacrifice to self-sacrifice, which may be meditated upon as a naked goddess beheading herself. Reciting Sanskrit verse, she aims spouts of blood into her own mouth and the mouths of her devotees. Goddess and devotees alike vomit out of time and space, spoiling the* anuṣṭubh *metre.*

Counting down to the dissolution of the universe . . .

1: To hum like shame

to be born and to be born and	to be born and other people	broken by have privilege hurl	the shameful parts | gods on earth ears filled with*aṃ* ||
live in objects interest gods	eat by kindness than cows service	backward acquire bodily in	entitlement | touchable my throat filled with*aḥ* ||
having the throat cover yourself	(Shyness as the worse than cows in	having the throat propriety	spirits inside | cover yourself broken by*aṃ* ||
by utterance what a pity!	he lives inside scheduled shudder	wear what will please bend the body	the hum of Fate) | belongs to him belongs to*maḥ* ||
wear only what possession gods	belongs to him don't touch my gods	wait only for having the throat	(Shameless as the | possessed self hurl offending*aṃ* ||
worse than cows in modest yourself	understanding untouchable	wife of Duty) destroyed by four	having the throat | white elephants self-possessed*aḥ* ||

2: To utter a joyful sound like will

what will not be will not be what |
undesired by doer of acts ||
eating inter constitution |
my only wealth morality ||
nowise able indeed to hurt |
for this cow is her enemies ||
inborn soulless owner's fine hair |
keep the peace self constitute ||
democratic birth conversion |
free debtor's entrance property ||
outer marriage choose their project |
etad eva hi me dhanam ||
withhold wishing boon to captive |
transmissible indeed to worth ||
walks like a goose turn delicate |
exo self rule small teeth you're mine ||

3: To praise like cover

'I am hiding something from you' |
euphonic tribes and conquerors ||
'from truth to truth' 'my body utters' |
as for ornament so for use ||
if the housewife does not sparkle |
the arrangement of a poem ||
growing 'what I hide by language' |
better colour aspirated ||
stressed reflection raw silk voiceless |
the homeland fails to be aroused ||

4: To praise in successive exclamations like veil

We advance pointing to our traces:
Inequitable lighting, unnatural flowers, the art of clouding minds.

'The marvel of the Indian shawl!' to render the wearer visible,
'The revels it has witnessed, all the torrid scenes!'

Black clouds to render the wearer,
Her dormant coldness of disposition, even in her own home.

Under no circumstances do we allow ourselves to be new.

5: To make a succession of exclamations like chaste

The crossed arms of Defence, the wide open arms of Need, the raised arms of Desire: a triptych of resolution. For among those who have made the resolve, the doers are best; among the doers, the flexible.

Sleeping alone, this sentence, uninterrupted, this merit, uncorrupted, this calm and equable body corrects. 'Upon my back, to defend my belly; upon my wit, to defend my wiles!'

'Why would a person get naked for a person with whom you do not share culture?'

[The gods have a duty: return earth to its constituent colours!]

[The unconstituted are entitled to compound brown arms!]

6: To shout like caste

a burn down*aḥ*!

ā remember*am*!

i entire past*aḥ*!

ī hereditary swagger*am*!

u previous owners*aḥ*!

ū collaborator traitors*am*!

ṛ fatal value*maḥ*!

ṝ dream learned and learned dream*am*!

ḷ pouring water*aḥ*!

e descent polluting*am*!

ai giving her away*aḥ*!

o pure death determined*am*!

au auto-erotic-decapitation*aḥ*!

am my mask, to defend my lustre*mam*!

aḥ and her, still bleeding, to profane all these*maḥ*!

7: To stop like cut

Indian Education Act 1835

'I have no knowledge of either Sanskrit or Arabic. But I have
done what I could to form a correct estimate of their value.' But
I have seeds, which would carry across seas of treacle and seas of
butter, which would resound for thirty thousand years. But I have
sounds, which would contain the distortions of their dispersal. 'I
have no knowledge of either Sanskrit or Arabic.' But I have taken
their throats.

'It is impossible for us, with our limited means, to attempt to
educate the body of the people.' I have taken their throats to form
a class, the first shall be the last, the first seeds last. *Satyameva
jayate nānṛtaṁ*: 'By truth is laid out the path leading to the gods
by which the sages', but in English, by which the sages are taking
their throats.

Their throats would move laughter in girls, their seeds. 'The sages
who have their desires fulfilled travel'; they are taking their gods,
their girls, by which the seeds travel. Truth travels alone, they
are taking their gods, but in English, they are taking their girls.
'This is proved by the fact that we are forced to pay our Arabic
and Sanskrit students, while those who learn English are willing
to pay us.'

I am having the throat. I am taking the truth to that supreme
abode of truth, 'a single shelf of a good European library'. My
shelves are poor and rude, my shelves are useless. The class
prescribes the class: 'I have no knowledge of either Sanskrit or
Arabic.' The interpreters who have their throats filled travel; their
distortions move laughter in girls, in gods. I am taken in English,
but not their English; my shelves line the path of resonance.

But I have heard them say: 'They want to take their place.'

8: To stupefy like bind

Indian Penal Code 1860: Of Offences Against the State:
Section 124-A-Sedition

Whoever, by words, either spoken or written, or by signs, or
by visible representation, or otherwise, brings or attempts to
bring into hatred or contempt, or excites or attempts to excite
disaffection towards –
'Her Majesty' – *aṃ*
'Or the Crown Representative' inserted – *aṃ*
utthāna, the act of standing up or rising –
'Her Majesty or the Crown Representative' omitted – *aḥ*
The Government established by law in –
'British India' – *aṃ*
utthāna, the act of rising (as the moon, as the disposition of the
moon towards self-rule) –
'British' omitted – *aḥ*
'Or British Burma' – *aṃ*
utthāna, the act of rising up to depart (as a warlike expedition, as
opening the door behind you, as welcoming ghosts) –
'Or British Burma' omitted – *aḥ*
Shall be punished with –
'Transportation for life or any shorter term' – *aṃ*
utthāna, the act of effort, manly exertion, evacuating (as seeds, as
stool, as gods, &c.) –
'Transportation for life or any shorter term' omitted – *aḥ*
'Imprisonment for life' inserted – *aṃ*
utthāna, the act of bursting open (as joy, pleasure, as safflower, as
proximate cause of disease, &c.) –
To which fine may be added, or with imprisonment which may
extend to three years, to which fine may be added, or with fine.

9: To paralyse like ban

Unlawful Activities (Prevention) Act 1967
Unlawful Activities (Prevention) Amendment Act 2008

To threaten a section
Hereafter integrity
jai bhīru, jai bhīru: our fearful beyond

jai bhīru, jai bhairava: frightful victorious
O Sovereignty
Secure in expressions of blame

Intent to strike terror
Prevention O timid girls
bhairava, bhairava: O reason with hunt

Have power the peaceable
Affection victorious
In behalf of commits any terrorist act

10: To expel like abandon

The Prevention of Insults to National Honour Act 1971
The State Emblem of India (Prohibition of Improper Use) Act 2005

Bastard saffron
Starve four lions
Loss of subtle
Mother passion
Trail in urine
Drinking *dharma*
Severed teaching
Horseshit triumphs
Can describe you
Red eyed gods touch
Half mast juncture
Subtle semen
Smeared with black bull
Meat salutes you
Disclaim ally
Accent value
Lotus weaken
Jayate white
Passion sewage
Dipping lion

Waist below truth
Petals browning
Satyameva
Her alone act
Selfish reader
Bubble duty
Vomit fondness
Source of pride their
Truth defeat home
Drape aroused freeze
Elephant head
Down this gesture
Menses *Mātā*
Outside smiling
Sunken eyes her
Gungey *cakra*
Righteous weakens
Saffron licking
Liberate shame
Bring her anger

Infatuation

The sacred fig tree, the branches of which drop shoots to the ground, take root and support their parent branches; one tree will cover a large expanse of ground, will shamelessly strangle its roots. Tremulous tree of wisdom, under which chancers sit, those who take root in the wounds of others, concealed roots, tension blossoms; those who fall in love like aerial dancers, accidently, not not taking flight.

Before Infatuation

no matter how much you
please you inherent

inevitable going
pretend adventitious
to design or to nature
we meet at take root

intensities border
little borders between
that which does not
exist red sap

you are going to smash

much you love

saps my

where one tense ends
look up
what does

cloud covers ground
break shelter pull back
than harder thins my

another begins

not missing something

cloud rests upon
peak acted upon

how we met in please

never imagined
can grow on another

at which of these points
should we say please
again please

mutual produced in
apply me authority

an appearance of strangling
an unusual part

neon refractions
false face must hide

wishing trees would

the happiest ever
roots fall from cloud

share under cover
at many points being

take sense
grow quickly

when the ground will be
same again
reached

to rigidity by
false representation
special expression
the more or less peak

fathom this sharing
the arms embracing
our origins in
where happiness ends

our dream dwelling in
collision of cloud

like insensible in
to the earth and take root

living on off or in

divination wets

enter the medium

can beautiful settle
the false heart knows

can air

should we say happiness
root in cloud

negotiate feels like
falling impose

deflect the course of the
drop to the ground

formed accidentally

which it may or may harm

love growing downwards
more or less than conditions

beside it grows
another
best

formed by roots
missing than nothing

like me

dreamed you

can put an end to

can whereabouts

prop descending

another begins

Infatuation

Beginning again, the goddess is rendered susceptible. Her body sets the coordinates of the whole wide world, but she herself is stuck: believing in the reality of worldly objects; watching the news; falling in the direction of the wound. She falls upon the grave of the wilful child, upon the raised arm of the corpse. A tree trunk stops five arrows. Sara Ahmed's rod as the will of the parent, our arms as life after death. Bhanu Kapil's mother's memory of a woman who had freed her arms. Nat Raha's arms kind and close arms, brown arms and private disarmed. The two of us with Sandeep Parmar with David Marriott with Suzanne Césaire's arms of miraculous refusal, talking, taking notes. This tender extraction of ourselves from our wounds.

mūrchana / making stupid

An unreasoning passion, an extra-
-vagant folly. 'I can't remember who
he was or who I was or what we did
or how.' A military show, her arms.

Making stupid, stand in business, 'by the
jingling of' class stupefaction in love
as the strong one 'their bracelets | as they bend
their graceful' breaking off their weakest arms.

Progress swooning your mother possessed by
origins exhibit origins
administrative affect 'a motion'
nervous 'to embrace' system of the arm.

Mind 'I went away and made you distant.'
A rise or fall of enjoying sounds 'while
our arms were busied' a noose a sword a
severed head while we confer boons in arms.

'The lotus stems' 'that built the house' what the
fuck you talking for causing inertia
'lotus stems' you profit allegories
profit 'when they become his' contract arms.

'They fly out of my' making fatuous
increase of fires in India they'd let
them all burn view from insensible swoon
'I dream of babies' with multiple arms.

Ignorance as the strong one: 'It's a sort
of wedding night.' You are very dreadful
as the horned one you look in a mirror
breaking the long bones of jingling disarm.

Good omen in women bad omen men
'the *Production* of Terrorism Act'
hand in hand combat public for granted
'stirs her will' overseas 'but not her arms'.

Golden state violence withered state love
'holding her legs up' demand and supply
stand well mother under collateral
pride of the rod curled as the hair bare arms.

'Will of the parent' waving from windows
winnowing baskets learned from the parents
'hands attached & gathered' produce neighbours
'dead labour' tongue your enemy your arms.

mohana / infatuating

The being deluded of assurance
infatuate national 'must take me too'
lovers not 'bothered to burn' divine arms.

Lovesick of 'the rod of the sovereign'
she sits on the rod '*of miraculous
refusal*' the paint peeling off her arms.

Blissful sounds mind I told you embarrassed
describe a 'graceful gateway' mind parting
mind melding unlikeness envy disarm.

'Her fill' of likeness thrown out the window
thrown into white corners her 'skilful stroke'
confers wounds fair-weather sister in arms.

Your children are browner your making light
'call them terrorists' brown 'birds mixed with men'
thrown against the wall you're twice-born of arm.

Your children are white like your fine armour
fathoming get to fuck measures of love.
'She stretches.' Deferring embrace wreck arms.

We are falling from clouds we are quick to
distance embrace former bump 'so tightly
she shall not go' mishear boop 'call to arms'.

The institution of their brooms 'exposed
as violence' feeding on enjoyment
of the earth kindness and kindness link arms.

Enjoying self as 'smooth and cool as pearls'
you come home to smiling to downcast eyes
gestures bloodied by the love in your arms.

Poor pronunciation of the greeting
smile 'they could not rebel' look down 'without
moral weapon' sigh 'they could not bear arms'.

mohanāstra / attacking

Attacking 'aliquots' passed 'like bricks' arms.
Against whom it is directed disarmed.
Water levels rising 'shades of' their arms.
Wounded pulling out of mind I said arm.
Fall on the pale of the ally cut arms.
Love in exile one to another's arms.
Constitute alien class confuse arms.
Social can get to statecraft attack 'armed
Neutrality' attack many crossed arms.
Irrational in bed fleeing from arms.

rocana / making bright

Radiant arm.
'Consciousness arm.
Of kind' make arm.
Can get to armed.
Fuck bright bend arm.
Twitching make armed.
Exciter arm.
Brown sphere fake arms.
Embrace disarm.
Secure stars armed.

saṁdīpana / setting on fire

'A gude' arm.
Setting arms.
'Cause maks' arm.
On fire armed.
'A strong arm'.
Failsafe arms.
Many armed.
Take brown arms.
Inflame arms.
Fall to arms.

After Infatuation

'Stars look like pebbles from here.'
– Don Mee Choi

when we were   skims and dips   projected
deathwaters modulating seafoam when we were   notknown
cast aside glance   dont listen to poetry
look allaround   elsewhere   are you island too
exclamation mark poetry   sunrising   listen to face
armpit speaks silver drips   good breeding thighs
governable eyes   speak sandalsmoke   nor quite concealed

moonlight becomes a   minimal beats bed sore
the breeze from the lily   downtempo   timely
tearstreak   the bright sky   honourably   handsfree   late
ah handsome waiting for   ah   turn slightest
becoming   inbox   all things for   doublehearted   her
ah magician   if you   but   sing standards
contradict loves nature   all inflections   for her

when love has reached its   timetoprepare   interesting
friends efforts bent upon bassgrind thrive posturing
peak preempt consummation   as if without you
as if fine   could this meeting   weakened
stomach rumbling hint emptybottlegreen distance shipwreckblue
     time
every syllable is flushed   comes back up
giddy sick between friends and lasttrain home

the world has nought so precious shoulders
pavement offers   restful from a portent ever
woozygolden first bus hope barearms kneebumps firstburpspromise
forget self wakeup   comes back upstairs   again
remember being shy drinkspill never jealous layitalloutonthefloor
ah horse cloud mountain   eking out genre
parkbench blink sosoon   into each others eyes

absent we set alarm clocks on fire
when near makes me offbeat   walkhome redbreached
seen steals away my self conscious   brownbird
heart when touched   puts pins in options
threecocktails blowupparrot the moments joy   warpface flirt
out my power   unpossess decided in advance
lost when you are lost what else

my   dust is somewhat   dressed down you
the flowers lie reddishyellowing in her hair
scatter powder lacquer footprints   lighted by serpentjewel
i kiss the cathair from your eyelashes
the pomegranate seeds   from yournomy mixedup memory
such is the poison she has taken
greenglow longing   turquoise dawning   these new infinitives

my love rests in my mind   asif
melted   restive therein   my horses skullrattle me
whiteface reflected or painted or sculpted loversmash
set therein asif jewelled everagain asif   nailed
loves five arrows   bloodstreamers   rosetting your heart
you are tightly sewn   into seven threads
looping separations thoughts loves continuum of everdotdotdots

Fainting Away

After viewing Arthur Jafa's A Series of Utterly Improbable, Yet Extraordinary Renditions; *after reading Emily Dickinson; after listening to Ornette Coleman* . . .

*

A gold and ivory mace was positioned in one of her hands, level with her cross-hatched waist.

> Your grandmother dreams of shopping for bridal jewellery.
> > I want to be ready for the last night.

An ascetic walked up to them in a smoky blue-lit cave. They didn't ask how long he'd been waiting.

> Your grandmother dreams of a future in which going home is not growing lean.
> > My ghosts will come before flesh.

Her face was blurred but the position of her arms suggested that she was smiling.

> Coming before 'vaster attitudes', you proceed from doubtful love.
> > I'm in without fading, mmm-hmmm.

The news ticker read: 'NOTES THROWN AT GIRLS DANCING ON STAGE.'

> You imagine yourself to be eye-level with girls.
> > Wanting my (eyes closed as empathy).

An ascetic warned them of the 'impending destruction' of ornately carved wooden columns.

> You call out your bad cause of a self.
> > Please stand up, please stand up, please stand up.

Five kings stood in a crescent, looking up. They prayed to a goddess for protection.

You don't want me 'so that the past could remain precarious'.

When she will ask me to-ooh-ooh.

A bearded man in pink and gold prayed beside a tree. He, too, looked like he was asking.

Nothing heals your father like you do.

Hello mister, ah.

Opposite, the silhouette of a goddess. She promised to take care of him as a daughter.

The second change, which takes place in warm milk.

Uncertain as to which of the two.

The newspaper headline read: 'Congress men for chemical castration.'

'What can I do my darling but try to speech' ghosts.

If I knew you were coming, I'd have tried to speech.

The big word 'honour' was pasted obliquely, issuing the smaller words 'police' and 'seething'.

Your heart from breaking our country back.

Hello mister, ah, how do you do?

*

Ornately carved wooden columns repeated themselves in a smoky blue-lit cave, issuing warnings.

The house that keeps your hidey-holes.

There, there, and there, ah!

A goddess held the heads of her enemies in each of her hands.

Your favourite action figures on the other side of the barricade.

Release me, release me.

Her skin became much darker; she took the form of their names.

You are hard upon anyone, 'So distant – to alarms – '.

And though my love is.

He said: 'HO! A MERE FEMALE!', foreshadowing his defeat at the hands of a goddess.

> To render downhearted, brown-hearted parenting.
>> And though my love is ooh-ooh-ooh.

The verb 'sprout' did not do justice to the sprouting of her arms.

> The frequency of your rage is not rage.
>> True-ooh-ooh-ooh-ooh-ooh yeah.

A dotted line was drawn down the middle of a devoted wife.

> How many of your lines draw attention to your body?
>> I won't tell anybody.

The sympathetic decline of his eyebrows was undone by the villainous rise of his moustache.

> Your visibility which is my seeingness.
>> My seeming this.

A state changed its name; the shift was equated with murder. The small word 'airlift' was pasted over a decision that deemed itself irreversible.

> To be out of breath (as lost futures).
>> Ah, ah, ah, ah.

She stood in front of a wind machine, black hair billowing under the 'scale of ill-treatment'.

> You return home to your favourites, they're waiting for you.
>> Ah, ah, ah, ah, how do you do?

An ascetic held the small words 'our society' just above his hands. Perhaps they levitated.

> You fall back into your stupid or slow elephant routine.
>> It ended when I lost your love.

*

The column of a devoted wife issuing from a devoted wife.

> You are indirect as an empty glass of warm milk.
>> How d'ya do, how d'ya do, how d'ya do?

A woman sat before a crowd; a ghost rose from a still-burning body.
    You fall back into bed, growing faint as the sound between your
    bodies.
        I wanted to be your, all I wanted was to be your, what do
        you want?

Eyes closed, lips parted; the subtitle read: 'world against'.
    You gasp for breath, as one who prays for exhaustion.
        Alone, poo poo bi doo.

The news programme was filmed in the business class lounge at Rajiv
Gandhi International Airport, calling aura into question.
    You just want to be as human as you can be.
        Alo-o-one, alo-o-one, alo-o-one.

A brown hand held a hairy brown belly above the big word 'gender'.
    Belly speak the categories of sound as not equal to the sound
    itself.
        Om Hrim Strim Hūm Phat.

'Ensure better' waits a while before issuing warnings.
    'An Unconcern so sovereign', you better stop.
        I'll proceed from unsuccessful love.

The expression of grief was 'on fire allegedly'; 'alone at home' took
the form of death.
    There's more than one way to find your way home.
        Fuck a home in this world.

A trident was poised to strike against a red and gold background.
    Your phrasing hardens, interferes, 'With Taints of Majesty – '.
        To cause to thicken, coagulate.

Her black hair billowing behind the heads of her enemies in each of
her hands.
    Wanting not to be sovereign (eyes closing as empathy).
        My cup of tea, my cup of tea, my cup of tea.

A goddess was told 'It's true.' Perhaps she spoke to herself.

    To speak from the low place, the promise of enchantment.

        My cup of tea, mine, mine, mine, you put me down.

*

The speech bubble read: 'I am ashamed to call myself "FORCE."'

    An image of community that you carry around in your head.

        The running around, because you're mine, the running around.

One king stood beside his daughter, looking concerned. They turned away from each other, but the small words 'blame game' acted as a bridge between their panels.

    An image of community that lets its children see it cry.

        I won't care, you won't want me, I won't care.

A goddess was crowned by 'SPECIAL' as she took the form of a burning body.

    You change together, you remember, 'For Arrogance of them – '.

        I'm yours, you're mine, we're going home, right now.

The newspaper headline implied an equivalence between identifying and honouring a victim.

    'You want somebody to pay you for your soul?'

        I love you, go home, I love you, go home, I love you, go home.

The newspaper headline implied an equivalence between 'PROTEST' in red and 'YOUR OPINION' in white.

    The image that's going to survive.

        Every sha-la-la-la, every woah-oh woah-oh, that's going to survive, right now.

A goddess said that she was omnipotent. The subtitle read: 'regular basis non-bailable'.

    You want life, you want spirit, you want less soil in your ears.

        Still shines, ah, still shines, ah, still shines.

An official said that marriage is conquered in battle, that concern is humbled pride.

    'An Island in dishonoured Grass – '.

        Just like before, so fine, just like before, so fine.

An ascetic warned them that accountability repeats itself twice.

    It's beautiful to go back home to where you come from, for yourself and for others.

        How do you like it, ah, ah, ah, ah.

A goddess pretended to be afraid.

    You've heard it all before, fuck a home in this world, over and over and over and over.

        I'll love you, I'll love you, I'll love you, I'll love you.

She pretended to ask for help, a gold and ivory mace poised below the speech bubble.

    To stop dying, to live again, eyes closed to solid and settled forms.

        Mmm-hmmm, from one dying to another, mmm-hmmm.

Death

from family, our seasons –
      – seasons we conspire for the sake of crossed paths

from the metaphysics of inheritance
    our dinner table training, our future-proof polish
        to the left, to the right of the shade

honey loving eyeing dying deaths of different kinds

I, family, am going to die; I will be hindrance

from the home of disease, the home of love
    our drunk eyes, our sandalwood dance moves

from the impropriety of multiple homes

all over the place folding back into thought
    – reflected in white granite –
        – tensile heartstring, *tulsi* putty –

almost always touching stretching thin folds back to thought

I, home, am going to die; I will be filament

from the hurting hold of here and there
from our remembered enemies, our interpretations

     – the state corrects itself, corrections restated,
   reinstatements posed
living bodies folded into the shapes of dead bodies –

> She puts her hands together, fills your mouth with salutation. Her hands part to pull dead bodies out of your mouth, your tongues, your mouth wide open as she ties the loose ends of your desires in your mouth, your other tongues, looping around her fingers, she knots your desires correctly, your loose ends dissolving, your hails of dead and dismembered bodies, her adornments, the parts of her body, her gathered bits, blood stickiness, golden threads, strings of pearls, hail choking, tolerance soaking, knots ending fringing pooling in your still opening mouth.

I, India, am going to die; I will be unqualified

from the sad smoke of our origins –
             – our safe distance, our wet socks

from the modernity of our sleeplessness
    polymorphous deities, sacrilegious throbs

that goddess doesn't mean what you think it does
it is further away than she looks

I, myth, am going to die; I will be slime trail

from meat, from wine, from carnal entitlement, from elective
emaciation

from decapitation makes your hair look good
        from squatting schematically, from *agarbatti* burns
                from painting lipstick on white petals
                        from applying white petals to purify skin
                                from plucking eyelashes, from translating
                                        sacrifice
                                        from making you – all the way – up

I, ritual, am going to die; I will be directionless

        from our well-formed, from our perfection
        – figment of millions, the passion of love, our great enemy –
                from generations of learning how to decline suffering,
                        conjugate illusion

        I swallow books upon books upon books
        to unlearn like-mindedness, to externalise cosmos

        another body grows inside my body
                – a statue of a woman, a veiled beauty, a hard-boiled egg –
        I am indifferent to the fires inside

        patience is a fully-grown body just under my skin

        wanting you –
                – needing this ending –
                        – dreaming of being decontextualized

I, Sanskrit, am going to die; I will be sunny-side up

from ocean, from abandonment, from unoriginality

from depending on the position of the planets, the explainers,
their promises
the nonce-borrowed defences, the walls they outline on your
belly and back

from your poster-paint instincts, your woodblock chorus
the compulsion to ask for help
      – green and purple neck feathers, dipped in saltwater –
        – liminal itch, driven to spurt –

from the severed totalities of other tongues, to the quick of being
recalled

I, dictionary, am going to die; I will be testudineous

from infatuation, as the condition of thought
to devotion as the current, rendering death

from my small steps towards you, tarnished silver
to my rubbings of the walls, around you widdershins

from your growing body, gendered by an accretion of touch
to your passers-by, unsexing the matter of your solicitude

from your three points, sinning religiously
to my fixed points, votive sediment

I, goddess, am going to die; I will be allergenic

from carrying across, a saviour, protector –

– the ripple of definitions
recollection a network of dark blue shrill

– a pearlwork of safe crossings
darkness an enumeration of her strung
stars

– her surpassing tones
accomplishment an end that she reaches
by falling

– fainting away
erotics a loosening of love's apprehension

I, Tantra, am going to die; I will be serrated

from the dead time spent apart from you,
spending lying die for you, the time of lying
alongside you, from the lie of dying far from
you, treading lengths apart from you,
measuring time spent dead for you, parts of
me die alongside you, dying me to write for
you, writing time the death of you, eyeing
me devouring you, timing me from end of
lying, ending you return to me, returning
time devouring you, time dies to elongate
death, longing to stop writing you, writing to
return to time you –

I, love, am going to die; I will be death

we are seen by the world / what must be seen

for Edmund Hardy

if we are seen by the world
small brown birds
finding themselves
making friends with hawthorn
hedges pluck buds
twist pearl on thorn blossom
pricks christen me nancy
why didn't you name me
name me nancy
writes poetry in secret
writes about gym pants
but I never write
(bookworm promises)
(crossing fingers at the origins)
never until
    mos and myre with clot and clay will cling
    mos and myre with clot and clay will cling
    mos and myre with clot and clay will cling
never until my accent
stretches to meet the premise of these chronicles

schooled in whose chronicles my own
heart skewered in whose gardens
I watch from the window
triśūla break lilac tree
liberate leaves
like heads heads like friends
old school ties
skew the whole world
cleave what must clag
keep porridge oats in lockets
(who loves you baby)

potatoes in bigger lockets
(who stomachs you baby)
my own sweetheart
assimilation cringe
slubbering in the peel
feeling up the wall
separating instances of not
not racist and not racist but
try denting the wall the view from the window

I close my eyes
to change the weather
as moonstone must
be seen to sing with spite
lappered thick
and filthily stinked
oh dirty feet blood-clotter
oh grease monkey clod-hopper
oh cloud-devourer spit
    out the tricks of the light
    out the dreams of bookworm-in-bothy
    outwith the hawthorn hedge
spiteful the noise
made by privilege
when boiling over
mess made by ejected oats
bitter the blout
breaking off the storm
it slushes the need for change
anothering blood rush out with force

half melted snow in the booth
foul the confession
every stage is a toilet
every reading a pot
for covering sounds
sounds like pearl return to clod

like talking about difference is
gludderly work
imagine a blue-sky brocade
shawl draped across
history's jelly slub
imagine white granite scaffolding
clatty lapse reactions
time sleekit to the touch
repetition transports
I start again
at the shared oranges of poetry and myth
my lubberly and delicate
common or garden variety
skin is no admission if what must be seen

Futures Flowers

You want to imagine futures. You want to create futures' objects
in your mind and to hold them there, until your mind turns into
the shapes of these objects. The practice of imagining turns into the
rightness of action, according to the metaphysics of the ritual, so that
flowers formed by the hands become the fruits of the practice become
abolition's efflorescence. The ritual must be repeated until it turns on
itself, its objects destroying their causality. You turn on yourself,
move into the void in yourself, and begin . . .

The red door to the temple is guarded by two elephants, both
vomiting rainbows. Their vomit meets in the sky above them
and fuses to form a lunette. The lunette is decorated with brides-
to-be standing a corpse-width apart. One is to be enjoyed; one
worshipped only. The brides are protected by lions, who are
nothing like the real police sitting across the street from the real
temple. They protect and enforce the reality that requires them;
you do not require them.

You prefer these lions who prop open their mouths with the
heads of your enemies. You decide to substitute yourself for your
enemies, abolishing liberalism by means of liberalism, placing
your head in the lion's mouth. Lying between the brides you
realise that your body is corpse-width; yours is the corpse by
which you must enter.

Past the first hurdle, you throw coloured powders at the space
where the door should be, trying to make it appear in your mind.
It's a jewelled throne on an island of butter in the ocean of milk.
It's a forest of the lotus of the heart that abides in the citadel. It's
a red door to a temple in the cremation ground inside your body.
Mind guards the door to consciousness.

The coloured powders fall into a geometric pattern on the ground of being and non-being. You lie down and puff your way in – it's easy! – you make it all the way, breaking through three straight lines, discontinuing tenses. Blow time out of mind, let futures flowers . . .

Another line appears, a dark line formed by a cloud's shadow. The cloud rearranges itself in the sky – it's an elephant, it's your mind stuck in mind – the dark line marks its time of death. The elephant bursts into hundreds of thousands of silvery spheres. You stand in the shadows, looking up, mouth wide open in awe of futurity. You swallow spheres, internalise obstacles that you may pass them through your body. Pass memories of elephants, pass clouds.

The line increases and covers ground; it's the side of a circle, accounting for error. The circumference is planted with golden arms, reaching upwards, stretching to hold each other's hands at the apex. You know there are no multicoloured hands across the world; there are oceans of wine surrounding mountains of flesh. Nevertheless, you visualise a circle of arms raising a cone of power, vitriol crystallising into bluestone. True solidarity is a beautiful and charmingly corrosive process. What if the future is faceless?

Return to the shadows. You project your shadows onto the clouds, casting your self-esteem, all those little mothers, into outer space. Mind-rays alight! Little mothers carry lamps out of your body and up to the stars. Infatuated with darkness, you resist their advice: 'Luminosity is the state of things that are luminous and also of things that are dark.'

You want to be left alone with your mind-rays, a cosmic puppet, dangling in the grandeur of the inner void, your desirelessness. But you are surrounded by kissy noises, resonating concentrically. Everyone and everything is kissing, except you! Your mouth is stuffed full of flowers and even these flowers are kissing each other, inside your mouth as if you were simply a space in which desire takes place. You struggle to imagine kissing from the perspective of your mouth. Your tongue is a brazen plate struck by lightning, and struck, and struck. You know that subtle sounds are better, unstruck sounds are best, and bite down on your tongue.

You bite off the head of your enemy and join in with anticipation. The cracks in the walls of the temple are stuffed with little yellow chrysanthemums. You remove these flowers and destabilise the temple in your race to one-pointed consciousness, which is the brain-facing lotus at the crown of your skull. The crown hides a hole, into which sky drips, feeding the thousand-petalled lotus that blooms behind and occasionally into and out of your eyes, your ears, your mouth. Feel the petals tickle your mind when you shake your head out of time. Feel the roots of the lotus penetrate the wet soil of sky and spread into the infinite wetness of space. No, not yet; the temple stands.

You must grasp the triangles, for one who is not a triangle must not worship triangles. The lines and angles suggest hundreds of thousands of awkward bodies, golden arms, sword fighting, sunbeams, laser quests, illuminated parts. But you strive for unbroken light, sectionless consciousness, sparkling waves of bliss.

The triangles exist in another dimension. They cast shadows in the shape of cubes in the shape of spheres, cast these shadows upon your body, cover your body in perfect solids. How absurd, the masters say, to spread perfection on your body like jam on bread. But you delight in hyperreality, this calculated immersion in pleasure, you pass yourself through your body without breaking your body, you make your shadows dance.

Your shadows hold hands, rub beaks, play footsie, wind tails together, totter rosily, cheek to cheek, bumpity bump bump

bump. They circle each other, full-body bobbing; they take each other by surprise, stand to attention, and stargaze. The absolute soul of the universe is an assemblage of migratory birds, whose agitation is indeed creation. You understand that when they say they dream to change the world, what they really mean is that they sleep badly. You say something about sleeping badly: 'The death of death whose destruction is liberation.' You say nothing about the seeds in your heart, the roots creeping into your circulatory system, the seedlings poking out of your centre of consciousness.

In truth, your desires are infinite, your actions infinitesimal. You are as close as you can get to the centre before sneezing, the temple inside you implodes in a mess of cremation ash, yellow pollen, third-eye twinkle and sonic dot. You are as far away as you can get from the world without renouncing it. Opposing yourself, you do all this as an offering to me, these flowers formed by the hands, this worship through the flesh, these lightning flashes of social life, this rhythm through rightness and opposition. You turn out of these objects, turning out.

4

Love's Future Is Death

6

Begin with Bhairavī, the fifth Mahāvidyā; she who sits quietly, reading and dreaming of devastation. Begin with inner heat, the righteous fury that accompanies slowly slowly studying.

*

Begin reading Fred Moten's *The Little Edges* in bed. Halfway down the second page, pause after reading the following lines:

> exhaustion makes life ever
> lasting. when I dance with
> you I am the moved mover.
> baby, you're a solid sender.

This pause may be imagined as a break before falling.

Exhaustion makes; exhaustion makes life; exhaustion makes life ever. Exhaustion is a drawing out or forth of air, of essence. Exhaustion suggests the study of multiple possibilities, the arrival at a single conclusion. This is study that consumes, conclusion that empties. The arrival may be weary, the conclusion weak, but it 'makes life ever' nonetheless. 'Ever' anticipates 'everlasting', 'everlasting' anticipates love.

'when I dance with', the space between me and you, subject and object, increases between us. We turn away from each other, we run side by side. To be both moved and mover suggests an affective correspondence, a rhythm that may be understood in terms of distance and dynamic: the transforming space between us, our changing positions. To be both solid and sender suggests direction, destination and promise, although not necessarily the promise of return.

Between lovers, exhaustion and solidity may signify the inevitability of tiring of each other, the perpetuation of trust in each other. While exhaustion and solidity are comparable in terms of constancy, they differ in terms of consistency – air and matter, essence and substance, breath and body – which suggests a certain equivalence and reciprocity of distance and dynamic. To be both 'moved mover' and 'solid sender' is to make life ever-changing, to agree that positionality is ever-making.

*

Begin by falling in love again, that which had seemed impossible. Fall in love with someone who isn't really there, whom I've never really met. Read poetry. Begin with indifference to external objects, because it's all in my head, it's all make believe, it's a trap laid by my enemies to keep me inside. Write! Begin by realising how much has been internalised: the painful process of deactivating traps for the sake of self-arming. Stumble over that line at poetry readings, whether or not I've scanned the room before speaking. Feel browner than ever before, and much less brown, and struggle to imagine any kind of future. Begin with headaches and missed calls and the demystification of memory. Reorientate myself to myself and to you.

7

Begin with Bhuvaneśvarī, the fourth Mahāvidyā, whose body is the earth, earth body. Begin with the place that I've been thinking about all along, my dirty feet.

*

In *Queer Phenomenology: Orientations, Objects, Others*, Sara Ahmed writes:

If orientations are as much about feeling at home as they are about finding our way, then it becomes important to consider how 'finding our way' involves . . . 'homing devices.' In a way, we learn what home means, or how we occupy space at home and as home, when we leave home. Reflecting on lived experiences of migration might allow us to pose again the very question of orientation. Migration could be described as a process of disorientation and reorientation: as bodies 'move away' as well as 'arrive,' as they reinhabit spaces.

The immigrant experience contradicts itself: it feels as if there is a home there and here; it does not feel as if there is a home there nor here. Moving between places, there is a feeling that something has been, or is, or will be lost. The body that moves between places is inseparable from loss.

How do I detach myself from the missing something of clouds? How do I leave behind the subtler clouds in bluer skies? Hail skies of grey, wind blow wind, rain down rain; the body loses parts of itself as it moves between places, between versions of itself in love poems and songs. It's not for me; it's not for me; it's not for me. You're gone.

*

In *Schizophrene*, Bhanu Kapil tries to write '*an epic* on Partition and its *trans-generational* effects: the high incidence of *schizophrenia* in diasporic Indian and Pakistani *communities*; *the* parallel social history of *domestic violence*, relational *disorders*, and so on.'

In the section 'Partition', she writes:

It is psychotic to draw a line between two places.

It is psychotic to go.

It is psychotic to look.

Psychotic to live in a different country forever.

Psychotic to lose something forever.

The compelling conviction that something has been lost is psychotic.

Even the aeroplane's dotted line on the monitor as it descends to Heathrow is a purely weird ambient energy.

It is psychotic to submit to violence in a time of great violence and yet it is psychotic to leave that home or country, the place where you submitted again and again, forever.

Indeed, it makes the subsequent involuntary arrival a stressor for psychosis.

In the section 'India: Notebooks', Kapil writes:

'Reverse migration . . .' Is psychotic.

The lines between places may be thought of historically and geographically. To go back to where you came from implies moving backwards in time as well as in space, from present to past tense, reversal as well as return, from here to there. The feeling that something has been, or is, or will be lost multiplies.

*

In *Black Skin, White Masks,* written in 1952 while studying medicine and psychiatry in Lyon, France, Frantz Fanon states:

Every time a man has contributed to the victory of the dignity of the spirit, every time a man has said no to an attempt to subjugate his fellows, I have felt solidarity with his act.
    In no way should I derive my basic purpose from the past of the people of colour.

In no way should I dedicate myself to the revival of an unjustly unrecognized Negro civilization. I will not make myself the man of any past. I do not want to exalt the past at the expense of my present and of my future.

For Fanon, disalienation, self-creation and freedom become possible when people 'refuse to let themselves be sealed away in the materialised Tower of the Past.' He is interested in the discovery of an ancient black civilisation, while understanding that history can obstruct self-creation as well as practical solidarity and commitment to struggle:

I should be very happy to know that a correspondence had flourished between some Negro philosopher and Plato. But I can absolutely not see how this fact would change anything in the lives of the eight-year-old children who labor in the cane fields of Martinique or Guadeloupe.

He writes of the wider stakes of international anti-colonial and workers' struggles, and, relatedly, of the feeling of being a stranger in the white/Western world. Yet he is most profoundly concerned with blackness. How, then, to think with Fanon while recognising and preserving our differences, specificities and the time and space that spirals between us?

*

Deferring Fanon's questions of solidarity, purpose and dedication, I ask: Do I move away from what comes before, or do I move towards what comes next? When I go back to India – historically, geographically, culturally and emotionally – what do I find? More importantly, what do I leave behind and what do I retrieve? What is the matter of what I choose to leave behind and what I choose to retrieve?

When I think of the Tower of the Past, it is inscribed with the script found on steatite seals in the Indus Valley, markers of a

South Asian civilisation thought to be contemporaneous and technologically commensurate with ancient urban cultures in Egypt, Mesopotamia and China. This script is not yet deciphered, which is not to say that it hasn't been translated.

The Tower is inscribed with Sanskrit, which sits very proudly upon the topmost aerial roots of trees, looking down like gods, as origins do. The Tower is engraved with warrior postures, chess pieces, unicorns and perfect circles upon lonely places upon noughts upon crosses upon crossed arms.

The Tower is built on the site of a mosque; it is built on the border between India and Pakistan, on the Line of Control between the parts of Jammu and Kashmir controlled by the Indian and Pakistani militaries. The Tower is built to distract from the dying and dead bodies on both sides of the border to which it calls attention; it stands to attention, casting its shadow upon contested sites.

The Tower is inscribed with an undeciphered script that right-wing Hindus translate as evidence of their divine origins, of their twice-born status and right to rule, of their racial purity and essential nationality. Right-wing Hindus instrumentalise the Goddess, in the form of the Sarasvatī River, to erase histories of movements and mixtures, as part of an ongoing process to displace and dispossess Muslims, Dalits, Indigenous people and marginalised social, religious and political groups, symbolically and literally.

Sanskrit is weaponised; its *aṃ*-s and *aḥ*-s that sounded to me like a chorus of laughter, a string of pearls, a source of pride and spiritual scaffolding, turn to bile and blood in my mouth, turn to dying and dead bodies in my mouth (the chorus sings: How many people died building the Tower?).

Drink water before saying her names, before praying. Rinse your mouth after singing, after eating. Spit after speaking, after praying.

Will you eat with me, will you hold me in your arms after I'm done?

Why do you hold me after you're gone?

*

Begin with the abandonment of shame, which means beginning with shame, being bound by shame.

8

Begin with Tripura Sundarī, the third Mahāvidyā, she who is beautiful in all three worlds. The most powerful gods form the legs of her throne, her rule is supported by men. Begin by wanting more for her; refuse the fallacies of representation and empowerment.

*

Sometimes, there is a desire that something has been, or is, or will be lost; sometimes, desire is inseparable from shame.

Begin by making a collage entitled '2nd January 2013'. The date refers to the death, a few days prior, of a woman known as Nirbhaya. She died in Delhi following a sexual assault. The materials for the collage include the *Deccan Chronicle* ('the largest circulated English daily in South India') published on Wednesday, 2 January 2013; screenshots of *NDTV News* (New Delhi Television) broadcast that day; photocopies of 'Tales of Durga' and 'Sati and Shiva' from the comic collection *Gods and Goddesses from the Epics and Mythology of India*; and screenshots of *Maa Shakti* ('a mega TV serial' about Hindu goddesses).

Begin by reading these mediatised words, which do not belong to me, in place of the words I cannot find. I want to find the words. This desire is inseparable from loss, inseparable from shame. I think about acknowledging this inseparability as moving closer to questions of solidarity, purpose and dedication. I want to find words to move close; I want to risk making contact.

Reread the collage and recognise that mixing visual and textual materials helps me to approach the sexual violence and structural inequalities experienced by women and feminised people in India, especially Muslims, Dalits and Indigenous, trans, intersex and non-binary people, as well as diasporic Indians, which I struggle to articulate in writing. The Goddess does not feel right in this context – what does she really mean, what does she really do? I invoke her and conjure clouds of smoke to distract from the issues of essentialism, superficial self-empowerment and identity politics that she carries, often put in the service of misdirection by gurus. I sneak her out of my critique, trying to keep her safe while I seek out her feminist potential, trying to make her matter without neglecting material realities.

Begin by translating the collage into a poem entitled 'Indifference to External Objects'. Focus on relationships between the gendered conditioning of Indian and British-Indian girls and women, and the colonial and postcolonial conditioning of Indian and British-Indian citizens and immigrants, in terms of submission, consent, dutifulness and desirability. By focusing on loss, desire and shame, I lose the Goddess, the source of my interests, translations and poetic practices.

Begin by remixing the collage and 'Indifference to External Objects' into another poem, another translation: 'Fainting Away'. This time, attend to the interrelationships between text, image and sound, and realise how much sound and music can do to destabilise such hierarchies of meaning and semantic value, as Sanskrit teaches me, as Tantric ritual demonstrates, as the Goddess knows.

*

I feel the violent and exhausting implications of my love and turn inwards to hide from my family and to avoid hurting anyone else. I hold on to shame with all of my arms, my two arms, infatuated with shame and unable to let go.

9

Begin with Tārā, the second Mahāvidyā, saviour, protector, emancipator. Begin with her safe crossings, her darkest blue.

*

The prefix 'trans', from the Latin preposition for 'across, to or on the farther side of, beyond, over' is etymologically cognate with the Sanskrit verbal root *tṝ*, which Monier-Williams defines as:

> To pass across or over, cross over (a river), sail across; to float, swim; to get through, attain an end or aim, live through (a definite period), study to the end; to surpass, subdue, escape; to carry or lead over or across; to rescue, save, liberate from

He defines *tāra*, the noun derived from the root, as: 'carrying across, a savior, protector; a high tone, loud or shrill note; the clearness or transparency of a pearl; a star; the pupil of the eye; descent to a river, bank.' The feminine form of this noun, *Tārā*, denotes a Tantric Hindu and Buddhist goddess.

Begin by understanding my translation practices in relation to this goddess, her denotations and connotations, and the ritual practices of her devotees, who name her over and over again: Lady Twilight, The Blue She-Wolf, The Dark Blue Shrill, The Compassionate One, She Who Guides through Troubles, She Who Dwells in the Cremation Ground, She Who Laments, She Who Carries across the Ocean of Saṁsāra. Tārā is evoked by the early usage of the English verb 'translate' in the sense of 'to remove a dead body from one place to another.'

Translation moves bodies, removes dead bodies, carries the remains of its histories and practices. The most special Tantric rituals take place in cremation grounds, which are ordinarily tended by members of the lowest castes in Hindu society. As Ambedkar explains, the caste system is the predetermined division of labour and of labourers and the preclusion of self-determination and social mobility, so that the child of the cremator must be determined by the parent and cannot be other than a cremator too (the conditions for other possibilities, if they exist at all, must be extraordinary).

Poetic translation involves attending to metaphorical cycles of metempsychosis and material realities of dispossession and death, which is where I want to begin.

10

Begin with Kālī, the first Mahāvidyā; she who devours time, she who expels black clouds from her body, she who dissolves the universe in darkness. Begin with the first goddess who is the last goddess; the death of my origins, my forever love. Begin with my dreams of being destroyed by love, of destroying love, of beginning again and again.

*

There is a curious association between clouds and elephants. Admittedly, they share characteristics – their towering greyness, their obdurate disposition to hold or release water – still they do not feel comfortable together. Something about the glorious earthiness of one, the frustrating unearthliness of the other. An unlikely myth reveals that elephants were once winged, roving the sky like clouds. They stopped to rest on a tree, beneath which the sage Dīrghatapas sat to teach. But the branches could not withstand their clumsy weight, and crashed to the ground, killing several of the ascetic's students. The furious Long (in time and space) Austerities cursed them, as sages in Indian mythology are wont to do. Now elephants can no longer fly or float or metamorphose, but their vapourish origins are preserved in language.

धाराट **dhārāṭa**, the Cataka bird (fond of raindrops) [proud cuckoo, only drinking water as it falls from the sky]; a cloud (filled with drops); a furious elephant (emitting rut-fluid)

घनाघन **ghanāghana**, (said of an elephant); compact, thick (a cloud); mutual collision or contact [another shared feature, the sound when they clash]

मराल **marāla**, (a horse; an elephant; a grove of pomegranate trees; white oleander; a villain; a cloud; lamp-black); redness mixed with a little yellow [a helpful definition or not, depending on how you see it; the components of a myth, whereby the horse and elephant are true friends who don't know it till the end; the scene is red with a little yellow mixed in]

मतंग **matamga**, 'going wilfully' or 'roaming at will', an elephant; a cloud

नभोगज **nabhogaja**, 'sky-elephant', a cloud

सल्लि **sattri**, one who is accustomed to perform sacrifices; an elephant; a cloud

श्वेत **śveta**, white, dressed in white, moonstone, 'snow-mountain'; 'a bright side-glance'; a white cloud; of a mythical elephant; of the mother of the elephant, after she died; buttermilk and water mixed half and half; in the evenings we played Eartha Kitt records, before returning to the brightest place

Notes on References

Here I name people, literary and artistic works, songs, places and conversations that have helped to bring this book into being. Naming is a ritual practice of invocation and exorcism. It is (mostly) in the spirit of gratitude that I name the following people and works, acknowledging my reliance on memory and personal records, and admitting that much remains unnameable. Page numbers are given for explicit citations (listed in full in 'Works Cited in Order of Appearance'), not for allusions, echoes, imitations, refusals and otherwise churned and charnel materials.

The epigraph, painted by Anjali Ramayya, is from an invocation to Vāc, the goddess of voice, speech, language and sound, in Book 8, Hymn 100 of the *Rig Veda*, as transcribed by Ralph T. H. Griffith.

1: The Goddess Disappears Underground

The painting of heather is by Jungran Kim.

Kamala: The names of deities are translated with the help of Monier Monier-Williams's *A Sanskrit-English Dictionary*. His voice can be heard throughout the book. *'missing something'* refers to 'Clouds' in Roland Barthes, *A Lover's Discourse: Fragments* (170). The 'yellow leaf' refers to Shakespeare's *Macbeth*. The stories of the Mahāvidyās, including the story of Satī, cite David Kinsley, *Tantric Visions of the Divine Feminine: The Ten Mahāvidyās* (2); Kumari Jayawardena and her citation of Raja Rammohan Roy in *Feminism and Nationalism in the Third World* (82); Kamala Subramaniam, *Srimad Bhagavatam* (68); Menon, Ramesh, *Devi: The Devi Bhagavatam Retold* (313); Roberto Calasso, *Ka* (84); Subramaniam (76); Kinsley (23); and B. R. Ambedkar, *The Annihilation of Caste* (233). D. C. Sircar's *The Śākta Pīṭhas* is a useful guide and enabled me to visit several sacred sites with my family, most memorably Tārāpīṭha in West Bengal.

Mātaṅgī: Samuel Johnson, *A Dictionary of the English Language*; Shakespeare's *Henry VIII*; Heinrich Zimmer, *Myths and Symbols in Indian Art and Civilization* (103, 70, 107); Sara Ahmed, 'Willful Parts: Problem Characters or the Problem of Character' (240); Johnson, 'Preface', in *Major Works* (323); Ahmed, 'Feminist Killjoys (And Other Willful Subjects)' (9); David Gordon White, *Kiss of the Yogini: 'Tantric Sex' in its South Asian Context* (304); Ahmed, *Strange Encounters: Embodied Others in Post-Coloniality* (39, 45, 32, 32–33); Mary Douglas, *Purity and Danger: An Analysis of Concepts of Pollution and Taboo* (199); and Julia Kristeva, *Powers of Horror*, in *The Portable Kristeva* (238, 241, 232). Sigmund Freud's *Civilization and Its Discontents*, René Girard's *Violence and the Sacred* and *Sappho: Stung With Love: Poems and Fragments*, translated by Aaron Poochigian, are additional references. Eley Williams prompted my reading and enjoyment of Samuel Johnson, and I am grateful to So Mayer for introducing me to Indigenous writers and activists including Daniel Heath Justice, Leanne Betasamosake Simpson, Billy-Ray Belcourt and Joshua Whitehead.

Bagalāmukhī: S. K. Ramachandra Rao's *The Yantras* informs this section. My translation of Bagalāmukhī's yantra is as follows:

Squares
Hail conjunction; oh hail pupil of the left eye; oh hail thunderbolt
Oh hail gastric fluid; hail competence
Hail soil keeper; hail self-control; oh hail churning stick
Hail wasting set free; oh hail rhinoceros horn
Hail leader of conjunctions; oh hail sky-waters; oh hail noose
Oh hail north-westerly wind! Oh hail horse unbridled!
Oh hail blockhead! Oh hail deformity! Oh hail sentences!
Oh hail possessing! Oh hail trident!

Petals

Hail prescribed knowledge! Hail terror of unbound!
Hail great good sign! Hail terror of universal dissolution!
Hail circumcision! Hail terror of death!
Hail pupil of the left eye! Hail frightful skull cup!
Hail boar! Hail frightful snare!
Hail omen in the upper sky! Hail limping terror!
Hail consisting of what? Hail terror glowing with passion!
Hail earth swelling! Oh oh hail formidable!

Star

Crack! Turn into a weapon!
Hail heart!
May blessings rest on the skull!
By the command of below!
Oh birch leaf! Oh guiding organs!

Triangle

Hail menstrual excretion; hail living in the dark
Hail led into darkness; hail deprived of eye's light
Hail speaking the truth; hail conclusion, for that reason; hail
as-so truly

Dhūmāvatī: Patrick Olivelle, *The Law Code of Manu* (96–97). The posing dogs are named Kulfi and Clipper; the lilac tree flowers in Glasgow. Thanks to my mother for documenting my performance as Dhūmāvatī, and to my father for providing AV support in the garden.

Chinnamastā: Olivelle, *The Law Code of Manu* (77). The image is found in Ajit Mookerjee and Madhu Khanna's *The Tantric Way: Art, Science, Ritual* with the caption: 'Chinnamastā, representing Devī in her destructive and creative aspects. She is flanked by her two yoginis, Dākinī and Vārninī. Under her Ratī and Kāma, the female and male principles, depict the transcendence of the phenomenal world and the abolition of the experience of duality. Rajasthan, c. 18th century. Gouache on paper' (84–85).

2: 'Is she anywhere after this, is she too far for us?'

The title is from my translation of the invocation to Vāc.

In the Rainstorm: Johnson, 'Preface' (324–25); Max Müller, *The Essential Max Müller: On Language, Mythology, and Religion* (93); Monier-Williams, 'Preface' in *A Sanskrit-English Dictionary* (ix); Monier-Williams, *The Study of Sanskrit in Relation to Missionary Work in India* (41); and Müller, *India: What Can it Teach Us?* (24). S. Radhakrishnan's *The Principal Upaniṣads* and M. L. West's *Indo-European Poetry and Myth* are additional references.

Out of the Throat: Sheldon Pollack, *The Language of the Gods in the World of Men: Sanskrit, Culture, and Power in Premodern India* (82). Thanks to my Sanskrit teachers at the Transcendental Meditation Centre in Glasgow and at the Language Centre at SOAS in London.

The Lexicographer-Priest: Johnson, 'Preface' (323, 326–27).

Notes on Sanskrit: Müller, *The Essential Max Müller* (246); John Woodroffe (Arthur Avalon), *The Garland of Letters* (216–17); Pierre-Sylvain Filliozat, *The Sanskrit Language: An Overview: History and Structure, Linguistic and Philosophical Representations, Uses and Users* (65); Chandra Rajan, *Kālidāsa: The Loom of Time* (110); Barthes, *A Lover's Discourse* (170); Frits Staal, *Ritual and Mantras: Rules Without Meaning* (116–17, 263); Jaideva Singh, *Abhinavagupta: Parā-trīśikā-Vivaraṇa: The Secret of Tantric Mysticism* (9); and Gertrude Stein, *Tender Buttons*. Paul Douglas's *Language and Truth: A Study of the Sanskrit Language and Its Relationship with Principles of Truth* is an additional reference. Thanks to my teachers, guides and peers in poetic practice: Andrea Brady, Vincent Broqua, Prudence Bussey-Chamberlain,

Sejal Chad, Robert Hampson, Kristen Kreider, Will Montgomery, Redell Olsen, Ryan Ormonde, Karen Sandhu and Jo Shapcott.

Notes on Tantra: White, *Kiss of the Yogini* (2–29); Hugh B. Urban, *The Power of Tantra: Religion, Sexuality and the Politics of South Asian Studies* (42–46); and Urban, *Tantra: Sex, Secrecy, Politics, and Power in the Study of Religion* (3). Catherine Clément's *Syncope: The Philosophy of Rapture*, Cecilia Vicuña's *Unravelling Words and the Weaving of Water* and White's *Tantra in Practice* are additional references.

Ritual Steps for a Tantric Poetics: written after attending Glastonbury's Goddess Conference in 2013.

Correspondence as Make Believe: written after watching *Last Year in Marienbad* with Diana and Gareth Damian Martin and Špela Drnovšek Zorko, and after reading Stefano Harney and Fred Moten's *The Undercommons: Fugitive Planning & Black Study*.

Her Voice as an Instrument of Thought: André Padoux, *Vāc: The Concept of the Word in Selected Hindu Tantras* (373, 377); Staal, *Ritual and Mantras* (261, 291); Woodroffe, *Shakti and Shakta: Essays and Addresses on the Shakta Tantrashastra* (427, 446–47); and Singh, *Abhinavagupta* (8, 76). Loriliai Biernacki's *Renowned Goddess of Desire: Women, Sex, and Speech in Tantra* and Jan Gonda's 'The Indian Mantra' are additional references.

The image is a reproduction of Bagalāmukhī's yantra, bought outside a temple in Hyderabad; the text is translated above.

Thirteen Days after Death: Manmatha Nath Dutt, *The Garuda Puranam* (766); *Bhagavad Gita*, translated by Swami Prabhavananda and Christopher Isherwood (82); Abbé DuBois, *Hindu Manners, Customs and Ceremonies* (548); and Monier-Williams, *Religious Thought and Life in India* (287). H.D.'s and Rachel Blau DuPlessis's versions of Eurydice are additional references.

3: States of the Body Produced by Love

The painting of a banyan tree is by Jungran Kim.

Joy of the Eyes: William Dwight Whitney's *A Sanskrit Grammar: Including Both, the Classical Language, and the Older Dialects, of Veda and the Brahmana* is a key resource.

Sleeplessness: Ambedkar's *Annihilation of Caste*, Diane Cluck's 'Easy to be Around', Lavender Diamond's 'Moment of Laughter', Fred Moten's *The Service Porch* and Virginia Woolf's *A Room of One's Own*.

Abandonment of Shame: Walter Benjamin's *The Arcades Project* and *Illuminations*, L. R. Chawdhri's *A Handbook of Palmistry*, Shama Futehally's *In the Dark of the Heart: Songs of Meera*, Bhanu Kapil's *Ban en Banlieue*, Thomas Babington Macaulay's 'Minute on Indian Education', Olivelle's *The Law Code of Manu*, and Shakespeare's *Troilus and Cressida*. The painting of rocks is by Jungran Kim.

Infatuation: The first section was written in Hong Kong and Brisbane. The second section refers to those named in the argument, as well as *Sanskrit Poetry from Vidyākara's Treasury*, translated by Daniel H. H. Ingalls, Kinsley's *Tantric Visions of the Divine Feminine*, Arvind Krishna Mehrotra's *The Absent Traveller: Prākrit Love Poetry from the Gāthāsaptaśatī of Sātavāhana Hāla*, and Arundhati Roy's *Field Notes on Democracy: Listening to Grasshoppers*. 'A gude cause maks a strong arm' was printed on banners at feminist marches in Edinburgh in 1909 and again in 2009. The third section cites Don Mee Choi, 'Weaver in Exile', in *The Morning News Is Exciting* (103).

Fainting Away: In addition to those named in the argument, Geeta Dutt's 'Mera Naam Chin Chin Chu', Britney Spears's 'I'm A Slave 4 U', Carpenters's 'The End of the World' and 'Yesterday Once More', Julie Andrews's 'Getting to Know You', Alice Smith's version of Nina Simone's 'I Put a Spell on You', and Mya's version of Dolly Parton's 'Islands in the Stream'.

we are seen by the world / what must be seen: *Dictionary of the Scots Language* and expressions heard from Dunoon friends are references. Thanks to Robert MacLeod.

Futures Flowers: André Padoux and Roger-Orphé Jeanty's *The Heart of the Yoginī: The Yoginīhṛaya, a Sanskrit Tantric Treatise*, Woodroffe's *Shakti and Shakta*, the Numberphile channel on YouTube, and Generative Constraints's 'Break Up Variations' performance and annotated score. Thanks to Eley, Diana, Kate Potts and Nik Wakefield.

4: Love's Future Is Death

The image is a detail from a Goddess temple in Hyderabad.

Bhairavī: Fred Moten, *The Little Edges* (4). Thanks to 'Race & Poetry & Poetics in the UK', especially to Nat Raha, Dorothy Wang and Sam Solomon, for helping me to realise my project, to find my people and to love poetry again. Thanks to Hamja Ahsan, Genji Amino, Tom Betteridge, Mary Jean Chan, Callie Gardner, James Goodwin, Edmund Hardy, Robert Kiely, Holly Pester, Derawan Rahmantavy, Preti Taneja, Benjamin Thompson, Laurel Uziell and Emilia Weber for conversations, correspondences, encouragement and friendship.

Bhuvaneśvarī: Ahmed, *Queer Phenomenology: Orientations, Objects, Others* (9); Kapil, *Schizophrene* (i, 53, 20); and Frantz Fanon, *Black Skin, White Masks* (176, 180, 176). Fred Moten plays a recording of Ahmad Jamal Trio's 'But Not for Me' in the background of this text.

Tripura Sundarī: the *Deccan Chronicle, NDTV News, Gods and Goddesses from the Epics and Mythology of India* and *Maa Shakti*.

Notes on References: The painting of jasmine is by Jungran Kim.

Works Cited in Order of Appearance

Monier-Williams, Monier, *A Sanskrit-English Dictionary: Etymologically and Philologically Arranged with Special Reference to Cognate Indo-European Languages* (New Delhi: Asian Educational Services, 2008).

Barthes, Roland, *A Lover's Discourse: Fragments*, trans. Richard Howard (London: Vintage, 2002).

Kinsley, David, *Tantric Visions of the Divine Feminine: The Ten Mahāvidyās* (Delhi: Motilal Banarsidass, 2008).

Jayawardena, Kumari, *Feminism and Nationalism in the Third World* (London: Verso, 2016).

Subramaniam, Kamala, *Srimad Bhagavatam* (Bombay: Bharatiya Vidya Bhavan, 1988).

Menon, Ramesh, *Devi: The Devi Bhagavatam Retold* (New Delhi: Rupa, 2010).

Calasso, Roberto, *Ka*, trans. Tim Parks (London: Vintage, 2001).

Ambedkar, B. R., *The Annihilation of Caste* (London: Verso, 2016).

Zimmer, Heinrich, *Myths and Symbols in Indian Art and Civilization*, ed. Joseph Campbell (Delhi: Motilal Banarsidass, 1990).

Johnson, Samuel, 'Preface', in *The Major Works*, ed. Donald Greene (Oxford: Oxford University Press, 2000), 307–28.

Ahmed, Sara, 'Willful Parts: Problem Characters or the Problem of Character', *New Literary History*, vol. 42 (2011), 231–53.

Ahmed, Sara, 'Feminist Killjoys (And Other Willful Subjects)', *Polyphonic Feminisms: Acting in Concert*, vol. 8, no. 3 (Summer 2010).

White, David Gordon, *Kiss of the Yogini: 'Tantric Sex' in its South Asian Context* (Chicago: University of Chicago Press, 2006).

Ahmed, Sara, *Strange Encounters: Embodied Others in Post-Coloniality* (London: Routledge, 2000).

Douglas, Mary, *Purity and Danger: An Analysis of Concepts of Pollution and Taboo* (Oxford: Routledge Classics, 2010).

Kristeva, Julia, *The Portable Kristeva*, ed. Kelly Oliver (New York: Columbia University Press, 2002).

Olivelle, Patrick, *The Law Code of Manu* (Oxford: Oxford University Press, 2004).

Mookerjee, Ajit and Madhu Khanna, *The Tantric Way: Art, Science, Ritual* (London: Thames and Hudson, 1993).

Müller, F. Max, *The Essential Max Müller: On Language, Mythology, and Religion*, ed. Jon R. Stone (Hampshire: Palgrave Macmillan, 2002).

Monier-Williams, Monier, *The Study of Sanskrit in Relation to Missionary Work in India* (London: Williams and Norgate, 1861).

Müller, F. Max, *India: What Can it Teach Us?* (New Delhi: Rupa, 2010).

Pollock, Sheldon, *The Language of the Gods in the World of Men: Sanskrit, Culture, and Power in Premodern India* (Berkeley: University of California Press, 2009).

Woodroffe, John (Arthur Avalon), *The Garland of Letters* (Delhi: Shivalik Prakashan, 2011).

Filliozat, Pierre-Sylvain, *The Sanskrit Language: An Overview: History and Structure, Linguistic and Philosophical Representations, Uses and Users*, trans. T. K. Gopalan (Varanasi: Indica, 2009).

Rajan, Chandra, *Kālidāsa: The Loom of Time* (London: Penguin, 2006).

Staal, Frits, *Ritual and Mantras: Rules Without Meaning* (Delhi: Motilal Banarsidass, 1996).

Singh, Jaideva, *Abhinavagupta: Parā-trīśikā-Vivaraṇa: The Secret of Tantric Mysticism*, ed. Bettina Bäumer (Delhi: Motilal Banarsidass, 2011).

Urban, Hugh B., *The Power of Tantra: Religion, Sexuality and the Politics of South Asian Studies* (London: I. B. Tauris, 2010).

Urban, Hugh B., *Tantra: Sex, Secrecy, Politics, and Power in the Study of Religion* (Delhi: Motilal Banarsidass, 2012).

Padoux, André, *Vāc: The Concept of the Word in Selected Hindu Tantras*, trans. Jacques Gontier (Delhi: Sri Satguru, 1992).

Woodroffe, John (Arthur Avalon), *Shakti and Shakta: Essays and Addresses on the Shakta Tantrashastra* (Charleston: BiblioBazaar, 2008).

Dutt, Manmatha Nath, *The Garuda Puranam* (Calcutta: Society for the Resuscitation of Indian Literature, 1908).

Bhagavad Gita, trans. Swami Prabhavananda and Christopher Isherwood (Madras: Sri Ramakrishna Math, 1974).

DuBois, Abbé J. A., *Hindu Manners, Customs and Ceremonies*, trans. Henry K. Beauchamp (New Delhi: Rupa, 2011).

Monier-Williams, Monier, *Religious Thought and Life in India: Vedism, Brāhmanism, and Hindūism* (New Delhi: Oriental Books Reprint Corporation, 1974).

Choi, Don Mee, *The Morning News Is Exciting* (Notre Dame, Indiana: Action, 2010).

Moten, Fred, *The Little Edges* (Middletown, Connecticut: Wesleyan University Press, 2015).

Ahmed, Sara, *Queer Phenomenology: Orientations, Objects, Others* (Durham, North Carolina: Duke University Press, 2006).

Kapil, Bhanu, *Schizophrene* (Callicoon, New York: Nightboat Books, 2011).

Fanon, Frantz, *Black Skin, White Masks*, trans. Charles Lam Markmann (London: Pluto, 2008).

Acknowledgements

Thank you to the event organisers who invited me to read – this book could not have happened without the space for experimentation and response that you created. Some poems were commissioned or written specially for events, including Sussex Poetry Festival, with thanks to Sam Solomon; National Poetry Library Open Day, with thanks to Pascal O'Laughlin; English PEN Modern Literature Festival, with thanks to Steven J Fowler; The Experimental Library at Cafe Oto, with thanks to Evie Scarlett Ward.

Earlier versions of poems have appeared in the following journals and anthologies, with thanks to the editors and people who work to bring these publications into the world: *Blackbox Manifold*, with thanks to Alex Houen and Adam Piette; *Chicago Review; Free Poetry: Contemporary Scottish Poetry*, with thanks to Peter Manson; *Liberating the Canon: An Anthology of Innovative Literature*, with thanks to Isabel Waidner; *Lighthouse: A Journal of New Writing*, with thanks to Jeremy Noel-Tod; *Nectar Feed*, with thanks to Ian Heames and Lee Ann Brown; *No Money*, with thanks to Danny Hayward and Ed Luker; *Orlando: Beyond the Body*, with thanks to Philomena Epps; *Oxford Poetry*, with thanks to Mary Jean Chan and Theophilus Kwek; *Poetry London*, with thanks to Sarah Howe; *Poetry Wales*, with thanks to Nia Davies; *Quaderna: A Multilingual and Transdisciplinary Journal*, with thanks to Vincent Broqua and Olivier Brossard; *The Believer*, with thanks to Sophie Robinson; *The White Review*, with thanks to Ben Eastham.

I am ever grateful to Peter Hughes for *Notes on Sanskrit* and *Correspondences* (Oystercatcher Press); to Jo Lindsay Walton and Samantha Walton for *In Me the Juncture* (Sad Press); to Sandeep Parmar, Bhanu Kapil, Sam Buchan-Watts and Rachael Allen for *Threads* (Clinic Press); and to Sarah Shin for this book.

Thank you to my teachers, my friends, Robert Kiely, and my family, named at the beginning.